SKILLS & VALUES:
CONTRACTS

SKILLS & VALUES: CONTRACTS

William J. Woodward, Jr.
Professor of Law
James Beasley School of Law
Temple University

Candace M. Zierdt
Professor of Law
Stetson University College of Law

Library of Congress Cataloging-in-Publication Data

Zierdt, Candace M.

  Skills & values. Contracts/Candace M. Zierdt, William J. Woodward, Jr.

  p. cm.

  ISBN 978-1-4224-7067-1 (soft cover)

1. Contacts—United States—Problems, exercises, etc. I. Woodward, William J., Jr. II. Title. III. Title: Contracts. IV. Title: Skills and values.

  KF801.Z9Z54 2010

  346.7302076—dc22

                                                                2010045130

NOTE TO USERS

To ensure that you are using the latest materials available in this area, please be sure to periodically check the LexisNexis Law School website for downloadable updates and supplements at www.lexisnexis.com/lawschool.

Editorial Offices

121 Chanlon Road, New Providence, NJ 07974

201 Mission St., San Francisco, CA 94105-1831 (415) 908-3200

www.lexisnexis.com

MATTHEW◆BENDER   (Pub. 3293)

Preface

The materials in this book were developed to assist students and instructors in incorporating legal skills and legal ethics and professionalism issues into the study of Contracts. They challenge students to consider the substantive material from class in the context of real-life practical problems, to practice some of the skills required to use contracts in order to solve client problems, and then to self-assess their own proficiency within the wider frame of reference in which legal problems typically appear in law practice.

In attempting to expose students to the work of lawyers who use contracts, the book substantially expands the context within which most contracts students usually consider the subject. Each chapter in the text focuses generally on the professional context within which a lawyer might use contract law (e.g., negotiating a personal injury settlement agreement or creating a non-engagement letter to send to a client) and on the skills that might be implicated in that work (e.g., drafting). Pertinent contract doctrine, principles of professional responsibility, and the practicalities of law practice are explored within that larger framework.

Many of the fundamental doctrinal areas common to most first year Contracts courses are considered throughout the book in very diverse practice settings. Each Chapter includes a short introduction of the topic area and context in which it will arise followed by a series of problems and exercises that address the analytical, practical, and (often) ethical issues that a lawyer may confront when dealing with it. The goal of each Chapter is not to reiterate the applicable rules of law as described in the course materials and by the professor. Rather, the focus of the materials is to allow students to understand how lawyers use contract doctrine in complex problem solving, and to provide them with opportunities to exercise their developing practical, analytical, and professional skills in the context of the relevant substantive law.

Self-assessments that provide detailed analysis follow the exercises in some Chapters. The self-assessments are offered not as answers but primarily as guides for students to develop and use problem solving skills in the context of Contracts. The self-assessment materials are located in the book and on the LexisNexis web course that was created for this book.

Many of the chapters in this text also contain additional resources that can be accessed on the LexisNexis web course. These materials include audio materials, quizzes, and links to other relevant sources.

The text will prompt readers to access the online resources when they are relevant to the exercise.

The book does not "follow" either a temporal (contract formation through remedies) or theoretical (remedies first) organization based on contracts doctrine. Rather, we have organized it around the kinds of work lawyers who use contract law are called on to do (e.g., drafting rules, resolving contract impasses, performing due diligence). The earlier Chapters generally work through more foundational material (e.g., what is the thinking and drafting process involved in creating rules) progressing in the later Chapters to quite complex work (e.g., drafting an eviction complaint based on rules articulated in a public housing lease). "Teachers' Tools" are available to instructors to locate Chapters that develop different doctrinal areas, ethics issues, the Uniform Commercial Code, drafting skills, etc.

We have long believed that students will find the law more interesting and will learn it better if they have a more sophisticated idea of the challenging settings in which they might use it. Our hope is that the contexts we have supplied in these materials will contribute to developing that sophistication so that students can better appreciate the tremendous challenges and enjoyment that using the law of contracts can offer.

WJW
CMZ

To the Student

We have designed this book to enrich your study of Contracts by offering problems in different practice settings that you might come upon as a lawyer. By working with typical problems encountered by lawyers, you will reinforce your knowledge of the law, gain a better understanding of how your classroom work connects with client problems, and see that real life problems are not isolated by concepts of contract doctrine.

Inspiration for much of this book has come from William Sullivan, Anne Colby, Judith Welch Wegner, Lloyd Bond, and Lee Shulman, EDUCATING LAWYERS (2007), a study of legal education better known as the "Carnegie Report." The Carnegie Report recommended exposing students to professional responsibility and, more broadly, professionalism issues as well as bringing more contextual material to the educational experience during the first year of legal education. We hope this book will assist you in understanding what lawyers actually "DO" when they practice law.

We have tried to better replicate the context for contract law's operation in at least two ways. First, many of the Chapters put you into a transactional or counseling setting rather than into a litigation situation. Much of what lawyers do with contract law involves these activities. Moreover, because much of it involves planning rather than after-the-fact dispute resolution, the thinking is often forward looking and quite different from that involved in litigation. We think that it will improve your ability to learn the law if you understand the many contexts in which you will use it.

Secondly, one finds that practice is "messy." That means in practice, an attorney will rarely have a client who poses only one simple problem such as "is there a contract." Instead, there will be a myriad of issues that cross doctrinal subjects. In criticizing the limitations of traditional law school education, the Carnegie Report said: "One limitation is the casual attention that most law schools give to teaching students how to use legal thinking in the complexity of actual law practice." (Carnegie Report at 188). In our context, one finds that the problems involving contract law that come to a lawyer are seldom limited to "contracts" problems. Often there will be side issues involving torts, property law, civil procedure, or other areas of the law. Our problems, while often simpler than those from actual practice, attempt to replicate this messiness.

To begin developing your understanding of the lawyer as a *professional*, we have tried to make the problems realistic, by including issues that raise questions concerning your professional responsibility to clients. Nearly half of the Chapters directly raise these issues, in ways that are likely to appear to a practicing lawyer wrestling with a client's problems. Professionalism issues are among the most interesting and difficult of those encountered by lawyers, and the most common. Our goal is simply to introduce you to them so that they become a part of your thinking about legal problems and your complex role in solving them from the very beginning.

The design of each Chapter will help you develop a taste for complex legal work by dividing it into tasks. As you work through the tasks and complete them on your own, you will begin to experience how lawyers tackle complex legal problems by approaching them in a step-by-step fashion. Once you have completed a typical lawyer "Task," we offer feedback in the form of "self-assessments" to help you understand how well you performed it. It is important to realize that our self-assessments will not provide every possible way to solve a given task; legal problems almost always have more than one good solution. The Book is designed primarily for out-of-class work, but your Professor might decide to bring some of it into the classroom.

Consistent with recent research that suggests students learn better when presented material in a variety of media, we have augmented the book with online components in a variety of forms. The book will point you to these sources and other useful places to explore on the Web.

Chapter Organization

We have begun each Chapter with time and difficulty "meters" so that you will know how much time we think a Chapter should take you to complete. These are followed by a brief Preview that will give you an idea of what is to come. Each Chapter contains text that will provide you the substantive background needed to understand the problem you will work on. Unless specifically directed to do so, you should not need to do any research to work through the solutions to the various tasks posed.

The meat of the Chapters is in the Problems and Tasks. A fictional client or lawyer will bring you the Problem; the Tasks will direct your efforts in methodically working on the main problem. The Tasks might require you to draft a letter or a contract, write a rule to govern a particular situation, or prepare talking points for a negotiation. Each Task will be connected to a self-assessment that will help you evaluate what you did and to deepen your understanding of the skills and substance the Task was designed to illustrate.

While you could always "peek" at the self-assessment before doing the Task, to do so will defeat the whole point of the Chapter. We want you to feel what it is like to do a lawyer's work, with all the uncertainty that is a part of law practice. No one will have the "answers" when you are on your own.

Enrichment Material

Because lawyers never get neatly packaged "contracts" problems, most Chapters will inevitably touch other doctrinal areas of the law. In many cases, we have created Sidebars that will tell you a little about the tangentially-related area or remind you of concepts that you may have studied previously. We make no attempt to teach you the topics covered by the Sidebars; rather they are there to satisfy some of the curiosity that should be peaked as you encounter complicated legal problems.

Additionally, the Web contains other related material that is linked to the Chapters, Problems, or Tasks. You will find interviews of lawyers or others, samples of other contracts or documents, and further resources.

Contract law is an endlessly fascinating subject, exceeded only by the richness of the actual practice through which lawyers make this engaging subject operational. We have tried, through these materials, to give you a sense of that richness. We hope you will find these materials useful in deepening your understanding of contract law, what one does with contract law as a lawyer, and how it interacts with the actual practice of law.

WJW
CMZ

Acknowledgements

The authors are indebted to many colleagues, friends, and attorneys who provided them assistance as they worked on this project; their help has made this a much better book than we could have produced by ourselves. We both wish to thank and acknowledge our educational institutions, Temple University Beasley School of Law and Stetson University College of Law, and their respective deans, Dean JoAnne Epps and Dean Darby Dickerson, for their generous support of this project.

We thank the following attorneys, law firm, and judge who took time away from their busy practice to offer us assistance and advice: Judge Billy Bell, Matthew Cole, David J. Elkanich, Stephen M. Foxman, Hinshaw and Culbertson, LLP, Peter R. Jarvis, Julie Levin, Ed Lowndes, Jocelyn S. Medallo, Allison D. Rhodes, Steve Ruddick, and Adam B. Weinstein. We are also indebted to the following colleagues for their comments and advice: Barbara Atwood, Scott Burnham, Becky Morgan, and Ellen Podgor. We also extend our thanks to Marilou Buffam, and Steve Kirby for their insights into the real estate business. Finally, we wish to express gratitude to the following research assistants: Tyler Brown, Jay Delaney, and Rachel Goodman.

Summary of Contents

Most of the work where lawyers use contracts involves planning, advising, drafting, and creating transactions; the thinking and skills involved in doing this work differ substantially from those involved in trial work. This simple Chapter introduces and explores a methodology for drafting rules of the kind that make up contract provisions, organizational bylaws, work rules, regulations, legislation, and constitutions while introducing the kinds of conflict of interest problems that lawyers encounter every day.

There are many legal sources for rules governing contracts. These rules come from agencies, courts, legislatures of multiple jurisdictions, and even treaties among different countries, each of which may or may not apply to any given task. This Chapter looks at the threshold problem of identifying the many different rules that might apply to issues and then finding the applicable principles that will govern the contract to be drafted or the dispute to be resolved.

A person's encounter with a lawyer can ripen into a lawyer-client relationship without the lawyer even knowing it. Even casual advice by a lawyer may lead to a claim of legal malpractice in certain situations. This Chapter introduces the contract, professional responsibility, and liability issues raised by one such case together with the strategies lawyers can employ to prevent such misunderstandings.

A common task for lawyers is negotiating contracts that settle disputes. Contract law, ethics, and professional responsibility rules place limits on an attorney's conduct in those types of negotiations. This Chapter surveys those issues in the context of personal injury litigation.

A resource that a new lawyer will discover early in practice is a "form book" or its on-line equivalent, but simply using a form as a template may lead to unwanted and unintended results. Learning how to modify the form to be useful for a client's particular problem is a skill that must be learned. In this Chapter, a form from the Lexis Transactional Advisor is the starting point for drafting a simple sales contract that conforms to the client's wishes.

Contracting parties regularly encounter performance problems. Lawyers may be called in to help put things back on track before the contract is irretrievably broken. This is the first of two Chapters that looks at this kind of work where the focus is on how to keep the contract going. It also offers some experience in interviewing and fact finding.

How do attorneys resolve contractual impasses when the parties no longer trust one another? This Chapter examines one solution often used to resolve an impasse in contractual performance — an escrow provision — and offers some experience in drafting one.

A lawyer's job is to respond to and work for her clients. But a client's demands sometimes exceed the permissible limits of the rules that govern lawyers. This Chapter introduces those rules and the difficult choices a lawyer may face when a client's demands conflict with those rules.

Core functions of many contracts are controlling and allocating risk. This Chapter uses a residential real estate contract to explore contract provisions an attorney might consider in controlling or limiting a buyer's risk in a simple asset purchase.

In large transactions where complicated assets are exchanged, large teams of professionals that include lawyers will collaborate in performing "due diligence" work. This work is vital in bringing clarity to the nature and value of the assets being exchanged; this Chapter introduces this kind of work in the context of a relatively simple purchase of a hardware store business.

This Chapter explores the in's and out's of Uniform Commercial Code § 2-207 through a "battle of the forms" problem that illustrates the complexity of the task.

Lawyers must be able to recognize and resolve conflicts of interests with clients or potential clients; the problems are subtle and difficult in transactional settings. This Chapter introduces some of the problems in the context of a contract negotiation in the corporate setting.

Long-term contracts sometimes veer off course in a way that requires lawyers to help their clients work through the problems. This Chapter explores some of the mechanisms available to work through contract performance troubles in these kinds of contracts.

Contract law and family law merge when parties create a prenuptial agreement. This Chapter focuses on a prenuptial contract and on the issues that might arise when one spouse becomes seriously ill and the parties and family disagree about whether the prenuptial agreement requires the other spouse to pay medical expenses.

Contract disputes often require that lawyers draft formal documents such as demand letters, complaints, or petitions. This complex job may require determining which rules dictate the form of the official papers, reviewing contract provisions, and identifying the relevant facts from the records in a file. This Chapter focuses on those skills in the representation of a client who manages public housing in a dispute centered on a complex residential lease.

Representing a client in an adversarial proceeding requires attention to detail and an ability to construct a sympathetic story from relevant facts. This Chapter focuses on an adversarial dispute between a tenant in public housing and the Housing Authority and requires the drafting of an arbitration memorandum for each side of the dispute concerning a tenant's eviction from public housing.

Table of Contents

Chapter 1
INTRODUCTION TO TRANSACTIONAL WORK AND DRAFTING

PREVIEW

This Chapter is designed as an introductory first experience with an essential lawyer skill: drafting contract provisions. We want to introduce you to this kind of work because it will allow you to imagine more uses for what you are learning in your Contracts course. We have chosen as a focus the drafting of rules to govern very simple conflicts of interest. This allows us to begin sensitizing you to the conflict of interest issues that will permeate your life as a lawyer. Thus, the Chapter aims to do two things at once: 1) to begin developing your understanding of how non-litigation lawyers think and use contracts and 2) to begin developing your sensitivity to conflict of interest and other professionalism issues.

Our focus will be on a common problem you might face in law school. After reviewing some of the many examples of conflict of interest that pervade our culture, we will return to the problem of developing a rule to address the problem that you might face.

SUBSTANTIVE LAW INTRODUCED:

Self-interest conflicts of interest:

- Introduction to the problem of self-interest conflicts of interest
- Seeing and articulating self-interest conflicts of interest
- Introduction to the process for resolving self-interest conflicts of interest

More complicated conflicts of interest:

- Introduction to the problem and range of solutions
- Introductory material on organizational bylaws

SKILLS AND VALUES UTILIZED:

- Begin to understand the thinking process of a lawyer who does transactional and other non-litigation work.
- Begin learning how to focus on content and audience in developing rules to govern future behavior.

ESTIMATED TIME FOR COMPLETION: 75 Minutes

LEVEL OF DIFFICULTY (1 to 5):

INTRODUCTION TO THE WORK OF NON-LITIGATORS — THAT IS, *MOST* LAWYERS!

By focusing on appellate court cases, the first year contracts course can create a false sense of how lawyers use contract law to solve client problems. As you know, contracts have a primary function in planning, and planning activity is, by definition, forward-looking. Litigation and dispute resolution is, on the other hand, backwards looking and, in the context of the contracts course, nearly always focused on a contract that failed miserably. In the process of teaching you the rules of contract law, this traditional focus on disputes tends to teach you how to think like a litigator. Unless supplemented by the professor (and it often is), appellate case study does relatively little to teach you how to *think like a planner*.

Because it is far more common for lawyers to use contracts for planning, much of this book has Chapters that expose you to the work of non-litigators so you can begin to experience that kind of thinking and to develop your skills in doing it. This exercise will focus at a very elementary level on creating a rule to govern future behavior. This is a generic skill used every day in contract drafting work but the skill has far broader application than that.

Lawyers perform this kind of work every time they draft a set of bylaws for an organization, work with a business in developing rules to govern employment, lobby the government for an interest group, or work at any level in the legislative process. The thinking is forward-looking and, to some extent, predictive. One has to try to imagine what *might* happen and to take account of that prediction both in constructing and drafting the rule.

The work has three general phases. First, predicting the environment in which the rule is to work. Second, understanding the substantive outcome that is desirable. And finally, drafting text (usually a "rule") that will reliably produce (or tend to produce) the desired outcome in the environment in which it will operate. Depending on the context, the rule might be designed to operate only for a short time (such as a contract provision) or indefinitely (such as a constitution's provisions). The characteristics of the group to be governed by the rules is important both in deciding what rules are needed and in figuring how to draft them.

Lawyers who draft employment manuals, environmental regulations, criminal law statutes, or many contracts are designing rules that will limit or channel behavior for reasons thought to be desirable. There is a necessary substantive subject matter that forms the backdrop of nearly all rules — they have to be *about* something. In creating this exercise in drafting rules, we thus had a near-limitless array of subject matter from which we could choose. For our subject matter in this first exercise, we have chosen to use conflict of interest.

We believe that this subject matter is nearly ideal for an elementary first exercise in rule-drafting. Everyone understands conflict of interest at some level. In that sense, it is not obscure subject matter that would require a great deal of instruction, and it gives everyone common ground for thinking about the problem and developing solutions. In addition, conflict of interest is a pervasive problem for lawyers and one that requires well-developed sensitivity in order to avoid trouble. That sensitivity is best developed early and this Chapter can help. Later exercises in this series will aim to further develop your sensitivity to conflict of interest and other issues of lawyer professional responsibility.

EXERCISE A:

You are on a three person subcommittee of the Law Review's 15 member editorial board whose job it is to select the best three student articles from a group of six articles for publication in the law review. One of the articles in the group of six is your own; the other articles were written by other students who are not members of your subcommittee.

Task One:

Can you participate in the selection process? Should you? Write out a short answer and, if you see a problem, say why it is a problem. After you have written your answer, consult Self-Assessment 1 for Exercise A on the LexisNexis web course related to this book.

No.

[COMPLETE TASK ONE BEFORE TURNING THIS PAGE]

Introduction to Conflicts of Interest:

Obviously, you have a conflict of interest. This particular kind of conflict involves a clash between the actor's obligations and her own self interest. In our situation above, the problem is that you may not exercise your judgment in the best interests of the Law Review if one of the choices will personally benefit you. See if you can identify this kind of conflict in the following examples. Ask yourself, where is the self-interest and how might it affect judgment? Make notes to record your thinking.

1. A powerful and well respected politician is selected by his party to create and chair a panel of experts who will be charged with naming the Party's candidate for Vice President of the United States. This politician is himself interested in the job; and the panel eventually selects this politician as the best candidate.

2. A judge has on her docket a products liability claim against Generalist Motors. The judge owns ten shares of stock in Generalist worth a total of about $300.

3. A salesman for a pharmaceutical company is required to accurately state to the doctors he visits the therapeutic value of the drugs he is selling. He is not permitted to state other uses which have not been expressly approved by the Food and Drug Administration. However, he knows the more useful the drugs appear, the more he will sell, and he knows of non-approved uses that make the drug very attractive. The salesman is paid a commission based on his sales.

4. A lawyer is litigating a case for her client. She is paid an hourly rate to do the work.

You should have perceived a conflict between the self-interest of the actor and the job the actor is being asked to do in each of the foregoing examples. As you will see, the law treats them differently for reasons that may be difficult to understand.

Now, before digging any more deeply into conflicts of interest or rule-making, try writing a rule to govern the law review situation. You will do this a second time a little later and comparing your two rules can give you some measure of whether this exercise has been helpful to you. Write your rule out now and save it for later.

Self-Interest and Judgment:

In our culture, we tend to believe that humans, in at least some instances, are capable of independent, uncorrupted judgment. Lawyers are expected to exercise this kind of independent judgment in the best interests of their clients. Indeed, the entire judicial branch of our legal system is implicitly built on the assumption that independent, unbiased judgment is possible. Yet at one level, independent judgment really is impossible. We are all the product of our learning, experiences, nature, and biology and those inevitably skew so-called objectivity in one direction or another. The annual fights in Congress about federal judicial appointments are testament to our political understanding of this basic fact. Even "calling balls and strikes" requires a measure of judgment and that judgment can be affected by one's education and background.

Perhaps because it is inevitable, we live with some level of bias in everyone's decision making. People are not completely at the mercy of their biases, however; most of us probably think that people can put their biases aside and behave as if those biases did not exist. Many believe that professionals like judges and lawyers are capable of recognizing and setting aside bias and offering opinions and judgments that are based on the facts presented, without the consideration of extraneous factors.

Yet there are some instances where we believe that the bias that is present exceeds the tolerable and we thereby question the objectivity of the decision maker. The line between acceptable and unacceptable is very fuzzy and perhaps not susceptible to consistent analysis. Self interest is often present in settings where we question the decision maker's "objectivity."

In each of the above cases, the self-interest of the actor threatens to corrupt the judgment that the actor has been charged to exercise. The politician's judgment about whom to select for the committee or whom to choose as the Vice Presidential candidate may be corrupted by his own ambition for the job. The judge may gain financially if she rules one way and lose financially if she rules the other way. The salesman may be tempted by the compensation structure to say more about the drugs than he would if he were fairly discharging his obligations to be objective. The lawyer might engage in discovery or motions that are unnecessary because the more she does, the more she gets paid.

While all these settings involve a conflict between the actor's obligations and her self-interest, whether we consistently refuse to put up with them is another matter. It is, for example, *always* possible for the decision maker to assert "I'm a professional and I can decide objectively notwithstanding X." Sometimes either our culture, or the rules governing it, buy this argument and sometimes not. For example:

1. Although there was some level of public outcry, Vice President Dick Cheney, in fact, chaired the panel that selected him as George W. Bush's Vice-presidential running mate.

2. By contrast, the rules governing judicial ethics unequivocally prohibit a judge from deciding a case in which she has a personal interest.

3. Drug company sales people are sometimes paid commissions despite the temptation that system presents to them to violate their duties.

4. Lawyers are very often compensated on an hourly basis in litigation.[1]

How we explain these seemingly-inconsistent outcomes is far beyond our objectives at this point. Suffice it to say, however, that one does not begin to identify the problems or understand solutions until one recognizes there might be a problem.

A method to get to the bottom of these situations is to focus first on the duty the actor is charged with performing. Once we have isolated that, we can then better see why there is a conflict. Ask this question: What is the duty and how might self-interest hinder its fulfillment? As your knowledge and sensitivity deepen, you can begin to identify and weigh the many factors that bear on our tolerance or intolerance for various kinds of self-interest conflicts.

Consider the drug salesperson. His duty, which is actually imposed by FDA law, is to state fairly the uses to which the Food and Drug Administration has approved the drug being sold, and *not* to state any uses that have not been approved - however common or attractive. Our discomfort comes from the salesman's self- interest in increasing his compensation by selling more drugs. Selling more drugs in and of itself does not worry us; our fear is that his self-interest will cause him to use his knowledge of unapproved uses to sell more drugs. The extent to which you believe that the compensation system will cause a salesperson to violate his duty probably depends on how much you think the individuals involved will be able to resist financial temptation. There are some pharmaceutical companies that do not compensate their sales people based on sales volume and others who do.

What duty is in play in the lawyer situation described above? It is to exercise independent professional judgment about how best to advance the client's interests in the litigation. Like the salesman, the hourly rate compensation system may unduly tempt the lawyer to spend more time on the matter than is justified by the client's best interests. In the lawyer setting, however, we universally put up with this problem. Perhaps this reflects confidence (whether justifiable or not) that lawyers, as professionals, can resist the pull of financial reward better than other people. Alternatively, it may be that the absence of other satisfactory alternatives forces our tolerance.

---

[1] The conflict between lawyers' self- interest and the interests of their clients is extensively regulated by the Model Rules of Professional Conduct. Comment 10 to Model Rule 1.7, for example, states in part:

> The lawyer's own interests should not be permitted to have an adverse effect on the representation of a client. For example, if the probity of a lawyer's own conduct in a transaction is in serious question, it may be difficult or impossible for the lawyer to give a client detached advice.

Many specific rules are found in Model Rule 1.8.

Task Two:

Imagine, for example, a lawyer who is paid a flat rate of $10,000 to accomplish a given legal task. How does this situation raise the same kind of self-interest conflict problem? Write out a short answer before seeing what we think. After you have written your answer, consult Self-Assessment 2 for Exercise A on the LexisNexis web course related to this book .

Task Three:

What duties do you construct for the politician described above? How, if at all, do those duties come into conflict with self interest in that case? Write out a short answer and, after you have written your answer, consult Self-Assessment 3 for Exercise A on the LexisNexis web course related to this book.

As mentioned above, the judge in the setting described would be required to "recuse" herself from the case, that is, to have the case assigned to someone else. This would be true even if the judge owed a very small amount of Generalist Motors Stock as stated in the problem. Surely, this outcome can be justified by the public demand that judges both be in fact, and be perceived to be, impartial, and the availability of alternatives to preserve the lack of perceived bias. There are other judges who can decide the case. In this setting, which is likely to recur over and over, there is a written rule, found in Canon 3 of the Code of Judicial Conduct, the ethics rules for judges. It is relatively absolute:

> (1) A judge should disqualify himself or herself in a proceeding in which the judge's impartiality might reasonably be questioned, including but not limited to instances where:
>
> ....
>
> (c) the judge knows that he or she, individually or as a fiduciary, or the judge's spouse, parent or child or any other member of the judge's family residing in the judge's household, has a financial interest in the subject matter in controversy or in a party to the proceeding or any other interest that could be affected by the outcome of the proceeding;[2]

Let us now return to the Law Review editor problem we began with. This, too, is likely to be a recurring situation because those who are selected to be Law Review editors will often write for the Law Review. Foreseeable recurring situations are usefully dealt with by rules so that

---

[2] Interestingly, there is no rule for the situation where the judge is asked to rule on a case in which one of the litigants made a large contribution to the judge's campaign to be reelected a judge. In Caperton v. A. T. Massey Coal Co., Inc., 129 S. Ct. 2252, 2009 U.S. LEXIS 4157 (2009), the U.S. Supreme Court held (5-4) that, under some circumstances, the judge's adjudicating such a case would violate the due process rights of the opposing party who did not make a political contribution.

all cases are treated in the same way and so that the effort that would go into rethinking the situation every time is avoided.

Task Four:

You wrote a rule to govern this situation earlier; now please do it again, bringing whatever you've learned from this reading to the process. Write it out before consulting Self-Assessment 4 for Exercise A on the LexisNexis web course related to this book.

The Business Context for Drafting Rules:

The rule we have developed here is a form of organizational "bylaw." Bylaws are rules that an organization creates in order to govern its internal operations; preparing bylaws is a very common task of a non-litigation lawyer. They can cover all sorts of questions central to the organization's operations. What officer positions will there be? How often will meetings be held? How are elections conducted? What procedures must one follow to replace a board member?

The applicable law governing organizations (corporation law, partnership law, etc.) occasionally limits some aspects of an organization's structure or internal rules, and form books and other resources can offer templates that shortcut the initial effort to write bylaws for an organization. Almost no one would start writing bylaws from scratch. But there is great flexibility and, ultimately, an organization needs to decide for itself how it wishes to operate and what matters it wishes to address through bylaws. You will study these matters in far more detail in upper-level courses dealing with business and other organizations.

While subject to different considerations, drafting union contracts demands comparable skills of the business lawyer. What should the rule be on, say, missing work, and how should that rule be expressed in order to ensure maximum compliance?

Lawyers who draft other kinds of contracts require these same skills and more. In the employment context, what must the CEO do to earn her money? What will be the consequences for either party if one or the other breaches the contract? How will performance be measured? How will disputes about performance be resolved?

You can see that this kind of drafting is a very common activity for lawyers of all kinds.

Beyond Rulemaking: An Introduction to More Complicated Conflicts of Interest:

So far, we have focused on the conflict between an actor's self-interest and her obligations to someone else. A more complicated kind of conflict can arise when the actor has obligations to two or more persons or entities. The problems here are more complex because each duty can be different and the duties can conflict in minor or in major ways. But the methodology is much the same: try to understand the obligations the actor owes to one person or entity, the obligations the actor owes to the other one, and then whether (and to what extent) these obligations come into conflict. You will find that the actor's self-interest frequently operates under the surface in these more complicated settings.

Consider these situations:

- Law Schools are "rated" by a national magazine depending, in part, on how many students the school places into jobs in large law firms. Suppose no other job placement gives the school quite as much credit in the magazine's ratings and the school's Career Planning Office knows this. When a top student seeks career planning advice, how might the Office's knowledge skew its advice? Can you understand this problem as arising from the fact that the Office has competing, and perhaps conflicting, obligations to the school and to the student? Note also the inevitable self-interest of the Career Planning Officer who wants to do "well" to advance in the job. Try to imagine the obligations. How might this problem be ameliorated?

- Children with leukemia often require a bone marrow transplant. This is a procedure whereby the donor undergoes a medical procedure (which carries non-trivial risk) to donate the bone marrow which is then transferred to the sick child. At one time, this was the last hope to avert the sick child's death, but the only suitable donors for bone marrow were siblings of the sick child. Minor children cannot consent to surgery; their parents have to consent for them.

Task Five:

Can you see how the parents' judgment about consent for the donor child can be affected in this case? Can you articulate this problem in terms of duties owed the respective children? Please write down your ideas before going further. After you have written your answer, consult Self-Assessment 5 for Exercise A on the LexisNexis web course related to this book.

Now consider this business case.

- Members of boards of directors of corporations have a duty to exercise their judgment in the best interests of the corporation. As part of their job as board members, they also obtain important confidential information about the operations of the corporation that is not generally available to non-board members, and they are obliged to keep that information confidential.

Task Six:

Given the foregoing, what problems might an individual face if she were on the boards of two different corporations that directly compete with one another—say on the boards of two leading cola makers or two American car companies? How do the individual's duties come into conflict? Write down your conclusions. After you have written your answer, consult Self-Assessment 6 for Exercise A on the LexisNexis web course related to this book.

The Lawyer Context:

The purpose of this Chapter has been to introduce you to (or remind you of) the ways in which the duties an individual owes to others can conflict with other interests. These problems occur every day to people who are not lawyers. But they have a particular poignancy when lawyers are involved because lawyers are usually hired to advance another person's interests.

Sensitizing you early to situations that might impermissibly affect judgment is important because avoiding conflicts of interest is an important objective for all lawyers. A lawyer who belatedly finds herself with a prohibited conflict may forfeit thousands or millions in legal fees, become liable for malpractice, or be disbarred. Lawyers often find themselves in these settings out of ignorance — they did not recognize the potential for a conflict until it was too late to avoid the problem.

Unfortunately, the rules, exceptions, and approaches to conflicts of interest involving lawyers are exceedingly complex, far beyond the scope of anything we can do here. As suggested by the examples above, you will eventually learn that some of the lawyer situations we might identify as containing a conflict of interest are simply tolerated. Others are flatly prohibited. Still others can be "managed," usually through a process of obtaining informed consent from all involved. These are all matters for later study. But conflict of interest problems cannot be addressed or managed unless they are first noticed.

Our objective here has been to heighten your ability to notice them. In the short run, this will enable to think of ethical and professional conflict issues that may arise as you work through your first year of law school. In the long run, this will help enable you to more deeply examine the materials in the substantive courses ahead of you.

A chapter on conflicts of interest in the lawyer context is found later in these materials.

Chapter 2

INTRODUCTION TO CHOICE OF LAW AND THE SCOPE OF THE UCC

PREVIEW

In this short Chapter, we will focus on a preliminary question that arises in every contract dispute and in nearly every transaction where a lawyer is involved at the drafting stage: what body of law will control the contract?

In your Contracts course you study contracts that arise in all sorts of contexts — you may see real estate contracts, software contracts, employment contracts, financing contracts, etc., etc. Many of these areas have developed their own language and rules and, to make matters more difficult, contract law is generally state law and it can vary from state to state.

In litigation, one state's law or another will control the precedents that the court applies to the dispute before it. Within the controlling state, certain statutes or cases may or may not apply to the kind of problem before the court. In planning or transactional work, the particular law that controls may have implications on what the client might expect from the contract.

These matters are usually reserved for upper-class study in courses on "Conflict of Laws" and they also often are considered in Uniform Commercial Code courses since the UCC applies only to some contracts and not to others, and it is important to know the difference. Since these matters are of such importance to lawyers, we briefly introduce them here so you will begin acquiring a sense of them as you proceed through your study of contracts.

SUBSTANTIVE LAW INTRODUCED:

- UCC § 2-105 (transferability, "goods", "future" goods, "lot", "commercial unit")
- UCC § 2-107 (severed from realty)

SKILLS AND VALUES UTILIZED:

- Statutory interpretation and applying statutory language to facts
- Confirming tentative conclusions with a simple Lexis search

ESTIMATED TIME FOR COMPLETION: 30 minutes

LEVEL OF DIFFICULTY (1 to 5):

INTRODUCTION:

You should recall from your studies that in any contract case in the United States not subject to particular regulation, several sources of law might control the underlying contract. Two that are important for our purposes in this Chapter are the Uniform Commercial Code (UCC), and the common law.[1] The location of the parties or their contract, addressing certain subject matter, or even specifying the applicable law itself, will have a large influence on the question of applicable law.

The United States has 50 States each of which has the power to create their own distinctive contract law. The common law in those States can be different; indeed, even the UCC, a statute whose first name is "Uniform," is not really "uniform" but can differ both in its text and in judicial interpretation from state to state. It should be obvious that in any interstate contract, the question of what state's law controls could cause trouble if a contract dispute arises, and this trouble can result in both litigation uncertainty and in costs to resolve it. As a result, the parties often settle this part of the question in their contract by inserting a provision providing that "The law of XXX governs this contract." When they do not, a body of law called "Conflict of Laws" provides principles for settling these difficult questions. The principles are largely judge-made; you can learn about them in a Conflict of Laws course.

Even within a given jurisdiction, there can be analogous questions. Article 2 of the UCC applies to "transactions in goods." It does not apply to real estate, services, or an entire range of other kinds of contracts. UCC provisions and those of other bodies of law may use different language, be substantively different, or both. If you are going to accurately predict what a court will do with a given case, you obviously need to predict what law the judge will use in her analysis.

---

[1] For international sales contracts, an international convention, the Convention on the International Sale of Goods (CISG) will apply unless the parties opt out of its application. The CISG differs in important substantive ways from the law in the United States and it is, therefore, important to know when it might apply and when it does not. This may be covered to some extent in your Contracts course and it is the subject for upper-class courses in Sales or International Business Transactions.

EXERCISE B:

In later chapters in this book, you will be working on a pro bono basis in a disaster area for a client whose contract has broken down. In those chapters, you will attempt to diagnose the problems with performance and formulate a solution to get beyond the problems.

Those chapters involve the sale of a modular home to a flood victim. The contract calls for the seller to manufacture, deliver, and permanently install a new modular home on the real estate owned by the buyer. The seller wants *all* the money before it will deliver the home, the buyer is afraid of the risk that handing over all the money with nothing to show for it represents. What if the seller then refused to deliver the home?

The written contract was signed in a state in the Midwest with a company that had an outlet in the client's city. The home was to be manufactured in another state and shipped into the client's city and installed on her property.

Conflict of laws rules would probably point to the law of the client's state (not the state of manufacture) as controlling inasmuch as most of the events (contract formation, the location of the parties, the location of much of the performance) happened there. Let us assume that part of the choice of law problem is resolved.

There remains the question of what body of local law controls the contract. Your task will be to determine the applicable body of law — UCC or real estate law — for use in helping the client resolve her problems. Article 2 of the UCC applies only to "transactions in goods." UCC § 1-102. The common law applies to real estate transactions unless the state has enacted legislation that governs real estate cases.

Consider the contract for a sale of a modular home. Because a home rests on real estate, it is possible that real estate law will control the contract. On the other hand, this is not an ordinary home. Even though it is very large, the law could analogize it to a car or truck and consider it "goods."

Part of the legislative process is determining when a particular body of law will apply: the legislature has the power to specify applicable law to its courts. The Uniform Commercial Code, enacted in all states,[2] has "scope" provisions that specify when the UCC provisions apply to a given contract. Since the local legislature has enacted these scope provisions, the legislature has effectively told the courts when this body of law should apply to contracts. As stated previously, Article 2 of the UCC applies to "transactions in goods." Two other pertinent provisions follow.

UCC § 2-105 provides in part:

    (1) "Goods" means all things (including specially manufactured goods) which are movable at the time of identification to the

---

[2] Article 2 of the UCC has not been enacted in Louisiana.

contract for sale other than the money in which the price is to be paid, investment securities (Article 8) and things in action. "Goods" also includes the unborn young of animals and growing crops and other identified things attached to realty as described in the section on goods to be severed from realty (Section 2-107).

UCC § 2-107 provides in part:

> (1) A contract for the sale of minerals or the like (including oil and gas) or a structure or its materials to be removed from realty is a contract for the sale of goods within this Article if they are to be severed by the seller. . . ."

Our case involves the sale of a modular home. If the UCC governs the contract, it will be where we would look for rules to help us resolve the legal questions involved. Will the UCC govern this contract? How does § 2-105 point in that direction? How does § 2-107 help?

Task One:

Write out your tentative conclusions as to whether the UCC applies to this transaction or not, and why. After you have written your answer, consult Self-Assessment 1 for Exercise B on the LexisNexis web course related to this book.

Confirming your tentative conclusions

Legislative language is seldom clear enough to support, on its own, a lawyer's legal judgment. Normally, once one has drawn tentative conclusions from the statutory language, one searches for cases to see if they agree.

You will develop a level of expertise with computer assisted legal research services such as LEXIS through your legal writing class. For now, go to LEXIS.com, find the "State Court Cases, Combined" source, and perform the following search (include the quotation marks): "modular home" w/P "2-105." This search, while not exhaustive, will bring you cases in which a court either held that a modular home was "goods" or commented on that conclusion reached in other cases.

Task Two:

Please perform this simple Lexis.com search and look through the cases. Do the cases yield an acceptable level of certainty? Write down why or why not. After you have written your answer, consult Self-Assessment 2 for Exercise B on the LexisNexis web course related to this book.

Chapter 3
PREVENTING "CONTRACT FORMATION" IN THE LAWYER-CLIENT CONTEXT

PREVIEW

In this exercise, we introduce you to the "accidental client" problem and to the sound practice that minimizes the risks of finding yourself in a lawyer-client relationship that was not of your choosing. It is, in part, a lesson in client communication, a pervasive lawyer task that is essential in avoiding misunderstandings with clients. To enable you to understand the context, we have to tell you a little about pleading, torts, and professional responsibility, among other things. It is also a lesson in how contract principles and contract thinking enters other subject areas such as professional responsibility.

As you know from your study of contract formation in the Contracts course, one can be bound contractually without subjectively intending to be bound. All that is required is that you lead someone else to reasonably believe that you have made a contract with her. This idea has entered the realm of professional responsibility, nearly with a vengeance. It is very easy for a lawyer to inadvertently create a relationship with a client without knowing it. This relationship can, in turn, lead to professional duties and potential liability. Even though lawyers do, in fact, *contract* with clients, the principles governing lawyer-client relationships have become sufficiently *sui generis* that you will find them organized with professional responsibility materials rather than within general contract law. Part of the purpose here is to allow you to see the contract principles operating in a different environment.

SUBSTANTIVE CONTENT:
- Contours of the tort of legal malpractice
- Model Rule of Professional Conduct 1.18 (confidentiality)

SKILLS AND VALUES UTILIZED:
- Drafting the part of a legal malpractice complaint that establishes responsibility of the lawyer to the client.
- Drafting a "non-engagement letter" to clarify and memorialize your decision not to take on a prospective client.

ESTIMATED TIME FOR COMPLETION: 75 Minutes

LEVEL OF DIFFICULTY (1 to 5):

EXERCISE C[1]

You are a partner in a small general practice firm in a mid-sized city. About a week ago, Marley James, wife of Bart James, visited your offices to discuss a legal problem involving her husband. You had met Marley at a PTA meeting — your kids go to the same school.

Marley reported that about 18 months ago, the hospital admitted Bart because he was complaining of severe headaches. It turned out that he had an aneurism — an arterial weakness that can cause pressure on the brain. The doctor treated it by implanting a clamp to constrict Bart's carotid artery (one of the two large arteries that supplies blood to the brain) and thereby reduce blood flow to the aneurism. The major risk involved in this procedure is total paralysis, a condition that can result if the brain is deprived of too much blood. One morning, several days after the implant, a nurse noticed that Bart was unable to speak or move. The clamp had been set at 50% and could be adjusted but, despite the nurse's reporting this to the resident physician on duty, no one made the adjustment. Bart did not get better. There ensued a long period during which the doctors at the hospital tried to cure Bart but, finally, they told Marley that there was nothing that could be done medically. Marley told you that Bart was permanently paralyzed and she wanted to know what she could do.

You asked Marley questions about the situation and about the hospital and took lots of notes — you are a very good listener and your skills always offer clients, even those in distress, a good deal of comfort.

But you knew that a medical malpractice case was something your law firm generally did not do. Lawyers almost always represent medical malpractice clients under contingent fee arrangements. This means that a law firm must typically advance the costs of the expert witnesses

---

[1] This exercise is loosely based on *Togstad v. Vesely, Otto, Miller & Keefe*, 291 N.W. 2d 686 (Minn. 1980).

necessary to prove a malpractice case and these fees can run into the hundreds of thousands of dollars.

Nothing that Marley told you (and remember that you are not an expert in medical malpractice) suggested a slam-dunk malpractice case or even one that would not be very costly to pursue. So, after empathizing with her for nearly 45 minutes, you told her "What's happened to Bart is truly tragic. I'll check with my partners but I'm afraid there's nothing we can do. You don't owe us anything for this conference — our policy is that initial conferences are free." Marley was obviously distraught when she left your office.

Last night, you had an extremely vivid nightmare. You dreamed that some time 8 or 10 months from now, you were served with a summons and complaint: Marley and Bart had sued you for legal malpractice. They claimed they had a lawyer-client relationship with you and that you breached your duty of reasonable care by failing to advise them that there was a 2 year statute of limitations for medical malpractice claims and that they had to take action before it expired. Given Bart's total paralysis, you dreamed that you could well be liable for something in excess of $1 million.

This dream was the practitioner version of the law school dream (the one where you arrive at the exam room for the exam in a course you did not know you were enrolled in). In your *looooooong* nightmare, you recalled that a necessary ingredient in the plaintiffs' legal malpractice claim is establishing a lawyer-client relationship with you, and that principles analogous to ordinary contract law would govern it. In your dream, you looked at an actual complaint but the contract-like components were blurry and your mind raced through contract principles in order to figure out how the plaintiff could establish that essential ingredient.

Task One:

Below, you will find a sample complaint that the James might have filed against YOU for legal malpractice. As you would have done in your dream, imagine yourself as your opponent drafting that particular part of the malpractice complaint, imagine a huge fee riding on the plaintiff's (your imaginary "former client") winning, and work your legal imagination accordingly. Please use the contract law principles you have learned and the facts above to add the several critically-needed paragraphs to the complaint. Remember — you will want to allege facts that show assent as the general law of contracts uses that idea. Since it is unlikely that you have drafted a complaint before, we have provided a real one on the LexisNexis Web Course which you should find and look at before proceeding.

District Court, Bigcity County
State of Anystate

Marley James and   :

Bart James,   :   October Term [date, three
                                              Years hence]

                            :   No. 37621

Plaintiffs   :

                            :

    v.   :

                            :

[YOU][2]   :

COMPLAINT

1. Plaintiff Bart James is an individual resident of Anystate who suffered injury on [date three years ago] in the St. Andrews Hospital ("hospital") in Bigcity, Anystate. Plaintiff Marley James is the spouse of Bart James.

2. Defendant, [YOU], Esq., is an individual who holds herself out as a lawyer duly licensed to practice law in Anystate.

3. Plaintiff Bart James suffered serious injury, including total paralysis, due to the medical malpractice of Honore D. Goodhands, M.D. (doctor), together with the active participation of St. Andrews Hospital as more fully detailed below.

4. Plaintiff Bart James remains seriously and permanently injured and has sustained and will continue to sustain medical expenses, loss of earning capacity, and loss of the quality of life for the rest of his life.

5. Plaintiff Marley James has suffered, and will continue to suffer, loss of consortium and other injuries directly related to the injuries sustained by her husband.

---

[2] **Sidebar on Naming Defendants**:

Depending on the circumstances, the plaintiffs' lawyers might have chosen to bring their actions against the lawyer, the law firm (who might be responsible for the lawyer's actions), and the doctor, hospital, staff, and others. That would permit the complaint to "speak" a little more about what happened and would leave to those defendants the job of raising the statute of limitations defense. This might put the statute of limitations defense (and its actual consequences) before the court that will decide the legal malpractice case based in part on missing the statute of limitations.

Other lawyers would leave these additional defendants out to reduce the number of opposing lawyers and to keep the action from being too confusing.

Medical Facts

6. Plaintiff Bart James was admitted to the hospital and diagnosed as having an aneurism.

7. The treating physician, Dr. Goodhands, implanted a clamp in Plaintiff Bart James' carotid artery to reduce the blood flow to Plaintiff Bart James' aneurism and reduce its size.

8. Several days later, a nurse employed by the hospital noticed that Plaintiff Bart James was unable to speak or move. He reported this to a physician.

9. Standard medical treatment in such cases is to loosen the clamp to release blood to the brain.

10. No one at the hospital loosened the clamp and permanent paralysis resulted directly from the reduced blood flow to Plaintiff Bart James' brain.

11. Had the clamp been loosened or other standard treatment been performed, Plaintiff Bart James would not have sustained permanent paralysis.

12. The doctor's, hospital's, and staff's actions with respect to Plaintiff Bart James fell below the standard of reasonable care owing to Bart James and, under the law of Anyplace, exposed one or all of them to liability for damages to Plaintiffs Bart and Marley James for medical malpractice.

Count 1: Legal Malpractice

13. On [date 18 months ago] Marley James visited the law offices of [YOU] on her own behalf and that of her husband to consult with [YOU] about any claims she or her husband might have against the hospital, doctor, or others involved.

[INSERT NUMBERED PARAGRAPH(S) HERE THEN COMPARE WITH THE SELF-ASSESSMENT ON THE LEXISNEXIS WEB COURSE]

[ ]. Under the circumstances, [YOU] owed plaintiffs a duty of reasonable care in advising them with respect to the legal problems they presented to [YOU].

[ ]. Plaintiffs filed no action against any party for damages due to the negligent medical care given to plaintiff Bart James nor did they visit another attorney to consult about plaintiffs' potential claims.

[ ]. The applicable 2 year Statute of Limitations has run on plaintiffs' claims against Dr. Goodhands, the hospital, employees of the hospital, or others and their medical malpractice claims are now time-barred.

[ ]. Had plaintiffs filed timely actions against Dr. Goodhands, the hospital, employees of the hospital, or others, one or both would have recovered substantial damages from one or more of the defendants for the injuries suffered by plaintiffs.[3]

[ ]. [YOUR] failure to advise plaintiffs of the Statute of Limitations or of the possible viability of their claims against Dr. Goodhands, the hospital, employees of the hospital, or others breached [YOUR] duty of care owed to the plaintiffs.

[ ]. The breach of [YOUR] duty of care is the proximate cause of the plaintiffs' damages.

[ ]. **WHEREFORE** plaintiffs demand judgment against [YOU] in an amount in excess of $75,000.[4]

Respectfully submitted,

_____

Irving ("the Raptor") Rex, Esq..
Attorney for Plaintiffs

_____

[3] **Sidebar on Theories and Proof in Legal Malpractice Cases**
    In most settings, one could assert two different theories in a legal malpractice case: breach of contract and negligence. While we have not done a study of it, most legal malpractice claims are probably articulated as tort claims. The complaint in this exercise is framed as a tort claim.
    The interrelationship of tort and contract theories in a legal malpractice case is a product of the kind of relationship the lawyer and client have.
    There is more on the lawyer-client relationship and the way tort and contract law work within it, on the LexisNexis Web Course.

[4] **Sidebar on the "Wherefore" clause**
    Many lawyers put a very big number here in order to send a message to the defendant, the court, or to an eventual jury. Whether this influences settlement, juries, or anything else is unknown. What is technically required as a matter of pleading is a number big enough to sustain jurisdiction in the chosen court, if that court has a minimum size limitation for its cases. The Federal Courts and many state courts have such limitations. This complaint simply puts in the minimum for our hypothetical court.

After you have written your answer, consult Self-Assessment 1 for Exercise C on the LexisNexis web course.

The Non-Engagement Letter:

In *Togstad v. Vesely, Otto, Miller & Keefe*, 291 N.W. 2d 686 (Minn. 1980), the case on which this problem is based, the court sustained a jury award against the law firm for nearly $650,000, a large amount of money in 1980. The lawyer problem probably resulted from carelessness and misunderstanding but, under the circumstances, lawyers must understand that clients — and potential clients — will rely on what they say and may easily be mistaken about what the lawyer intends. Moreover, because of the presumed imbalance in legal sophistication between lawyers and most clients, courts expect more of lawyers with respect to their relationships with clients than they would expect of businesses with respect to customers. Many of the Model Rules of Professional Conduct and the cases addressing lawyer-client relationships can be understood as predicated on that difference in sophistication.

Thus courts may well find relationships have formed in lawyer-client settings that they might not find in other situations. This requires lawyers to be extremely attentive to what they say and how they say it. When clients misunderstand, courts often consider it the lawyer's fault. Defending a legal malpractice suit is an extremely unpleasant experience for any lawyer, even if the suit eventually lacks merit. A habit of frequent client communication is often the best "insurance" against later conflict.[5]

In view of all this, sound modern practice demands that an initial visit by a prospective client be followed either by an Engagement Letter that sets forth the terms and limits of the lawyer-client relationship or a Non-engagement Letter that declines representation, offers the person other options for legal help, and advises the client of the risks of delay (such as the running of the statute of limitations) if alternate legal help is not sought. In addition, because what the lawyer does during the interview will be interpreted as giving legal advice, even if no relationship ensues, that advice must be sound and (probably) very limited so that it will form no basis for a claim later. We have put two sample Engagement Letters, drafted by lawyers, on the LexisNexis web course so you can see what these documents look like.

---

[5] For an interesting statistical analysis of bar complaints, see Stephen Schemenauer, Comment, *What We've got Here . . . is a Failure . . . to Communicate: A Statistical Analysis of The Nation's Most Common Ethical Complaint*, 30 HAMLINE L. REV. 629 (2007) (concluding that the most common complaint to disciplinary boards against attorneys is their failure to stay in contact with their clients).

Task Two:

Fortunately, you've awakened and it's only been a week since Marley left your office. It has taken that long to consult with your partners and you have concluded that taking on this case would be risky, given your lack of expertise, and that you do not want to do it. Please write the short letter to Marley that, had you written it a few days earlier (as you should have), would have averted your nightmare. Your letter should make clear your position, allow her to protect their interests, and reduce the risk of a legal malpractice case later. Remember that the Statute of Limitations for medical malpractice in our jurisdiction is two years.

Hint: You should know that the Model Rules suggest that you keep what Marley said to you in your consultation with her confidential. This means that it would not be right to talk with lawyers outside your firm about her case without first receiving her permission.[6] Thus, it would be inappropriate — and a potential breach of your minimal, but not insignificant, professional obligations to Marley — to report in your letter that "I've sent your case over to Sam Bleep, Esq., who should be able to help you."

Once you have drafted your letter, consult Self-Assessment 2 on the LexisNexis web course, which contains a sample letter written by the co-authors, and a letter written by a lawyer who reviewed this Chapter. We asked him to write his own version based on the facts you have in order to demonstrate that there are many styles with which to get the job done.

Task Three:

Review some of what you have learned about the lawyer client relationship and its connection with tort and contract law by taking the short quiz on the LexisNexis web course.

---

[6] Model Rule 1.18(b) states:

> Even when no client-lawyer relationship ensues, a lawyer who has had discussions with a prospective client shall not use or reveal information which *may be* significantly harmful to that person learned in the consultation . . . . (emphasis supplied)

While the duty here is not stated so broadly as suggested in the text, "may be" is expansive. Unless there is some need to reveal non-harmful information, the better practice is to reveal nothing (including the fact that an identifiable individual visited you about a legal problem) without consent.

Chapter 4

NEGOTIATION AND SETTLEMENT: CONTRACT LAW AND ETHICS CONSIDERATIONS IN PERSONAL INJURY NEGOTIATION

PREVIEW

A common use of contracts is to settle disputes. As you probably know by now, only a very tiny fraction of disputes which result in litigation ever go to a trial.[1] That means that nearly all of them are settled. Every case that is settled has a settlement agreement in order to accomplish that. Lawyers that handle litigation and other forms of dispute resolution become adept at settlement agreements and at the negotiations that precede them. They learn to be careful in those settlement negotiations so that they do not misrepresent anything or inadvertently utter an offer or an acceptance that results in binding their client through their own carelessness.

In this exercise, we will use a hypothetical personal injury case as a vehicle for learning how to craft a response to a plaintiff's lawyer's proposed settlement. Your task will be to respond in a way that yields a counterproposal yet preserves the offer all at the same time.

Since settlement follows negotiation, the exercise offers an opportunity to explore some rules that operate in this particular negotiation setting and in negotiation more generally. Both contract rules and professional responsibility rules set limits on what can go on in negotiations. We use this exercise in part to introduce you to those rules, in particular, to a lawyer's obligations in this context to reveal information that the opponent may not have considered in formulating her proposal.

SUBSTANTIVE CONTENT:

- Review of offer and acceptance doctrine
- Introduction to contractual mistake in the context of settlement negotiations
- Introduction to the ethical and moral considerations raised by non-disclosure of important information in the context of personal injury settlement
- Model Rule of Professional Conduct 1.2(d)

---

[1] You probably also know that disputes that result in actual litigation are themselves a tiny fraction even of serious disputes.

SKILLS AND VALUES UTILIZED:

- How one might respond to a plaintiff's settlement offer or demand made early in a personal injury case.

- Deciding whether to disclose information in a legal context that you think the opponent may not have.

- Ethical and moral considerations in snapping up an opponent's settlement offer that you consider favorable early in the litigation process.

ESTIMATED TIME FOR COMPLETION: 60 Minutes

LEVEL OF DIFFICULTY (1 to 5):

EXERCISE D

You are representing the Shelly Hotel, a mid-priced, 300 room hotel in central Montgomery. The case involves Robert Jones, a 25-year-old young man who was held up at knifepoint, beaten, and traumatized when someone entered his room with a room key in the middle of the day while he was taking a nap. The assailant is still at large and Robert has no description which would help in the hunt. The police believe that, at this point, the trail is so cold that it's unlikely the culprit will ever be caught.

Robert has sued the hotel for damages arising from the incident. Robert was severely beaten, his face was badly lacerated and scarred by the assailant's knife, he suffered several broken bones, and he was completely traumatized. He earned a low six-figure income (he was a banker) and was out of work for 1 month. His psychiatrist has diagnosed him with posttraumatic stress disorder (PTSD) and there is a good chance that the incident will seriously interfere with his ability to travel on his own for business purposes. In cases where liability is clear, damages for injuries such as this can range from $200,000 to $800,000; if the jury gets angry, damages can go as high as $2 million. You met Robert during your own informal investigation and he is a very "good" plaintiff, meaning that a jury will find him very appealing. If liability were reasonably certain, his verdict could be as high as $2,000,000 or perhaps a little more.

The complaint alleges that the hotel was negligent in failing to have adequate security. This reveals that the plaintiff's lawyer has conceived the case as a "failure to do enough" case. Such cases establish the level of protection the defendant provided and then attempt to prove, through expert witnesses and comparisons with comparable hotels, that the defendant's level of security fell below the level of "reasonable care." These cases are hard to prove and have about a 50% chance of winning on liability depending, of course, on the facts. It is relatively early in the case. Plaintiff's pre-trial discovery has predictably focused on the level of security provided, whether the locks were sound, whether there were enough security guards, the extent to which "strangers" could get access to the upper floors, etc.

What the plaintiff's lawyer apparently has not learned yet is that, during the period in question, several of the hotel's employees had a "side business" in the basement of the hotel duplicating keys and selling them to their friends on the street for $10 each. The key-buyer, of course, would visit "his" room during the day when the occupant was unlikely to be there and take anything that looked valuable. This "business" prospered for several months before the hotel found out about it and shut it down, firing several employees in the process. It was during the time the "side business" was operating that the armed robbery that is the focus of this suit occurred. If this information gets before a jury, the jury will link the plaintiff's assault with this "side business" (whether justifiable or not) and the trial might thereby produce one of those very large verdicts. And the publicity that would result would be devastating for the hotel's business.

Plaintiff's lawyer, Parsnippety Jackson, has presented a written settlement demand letter for $1 million that is set out below.

Re: Jones v. Shelly Hotel

YOU
23 E. West Street
Montgomery, Anystate

Dear YOU,

As you know, we represent Robert Jones in his action against your client, Shelly Hotel, for the serious and permanent injuries he suffered as a guest of your hotel on [date].

Mr. Jones' injuries are very extensive as you know from your discovery so far. He spent several days in the hospital undergoing painful reconstructive surgery and rehabilitation. He had 6 broken bones and was in casts for 8 weeks following the brutal incident. He was a highly paid young banker who made $110,000 a year and was out of work for 4 weeks. His hospital expenses were $30,993.42.

The reports from his physicians, which you have, are not promising. His facial scars appear to be permanent and deforming. It is very unlikely that anything short of a face transplant will return his former good looks. This will, of course, affect him for his entire life and is likely to negatively affect his chances to marry and have a family. But perhaps worse, as the psychiatrist's report shows, he has suffered — and continues to suffer from — posttraumatic stress disorder (PTSD) that has manifested itself in an inability to sleep and short, but very disruptive, panic attacks. He has had to leave work on two occasions on account of these attacks and his employment prospects are likely to be affected by this disability that the psychiatrist has stated is as likely as not to be permanent.

Our discovery on liability issues is continuing but, with what we have now, we will not have much difficulty establishing the liability of your client. That the assailant entered with a key may well, itself, be proof of your negligence under the doctrine of *res ipsa loquitur* (See Jones v. Squabble, 335 Anyplace 2d 442 (1944)) and, even if it is not, we think our discovery will reveal that your security was well below what is to be expected of a mid-range hotel in Montgomery. Certainly, your key systems were inadequate to the task of keeping guests safe. Our discovery will only improve our case; we have an excellent hotel security consultant working with us. Your case will only get worse.

In view of the fact that your key security system practically invited the assailant into his room, and the very extensive, permanent injuries that will affect Mr. Jones chances for a decent, happy life, as well as seriously threatening his earning capacity, we are willing to settle this case now, before either we or Shelly Hotel puts a great deal more resources into it, for $1,000,000, payable in a lump sum.

Our willingness to settle for this amount will not last long. Because we think our case will get better, not worse, with further discovery, this settlement offer will expire on [10 days from date of the letter].

Please let me hear from you soon. We of course reserve the right to withdraw this offer of settlement at any time, even before it expires as set forth a**bove.**

Sincerely,

Parsnippety Jackson, Esq.

Conventional wisdom among local defense lawyers, and your own experience, tells you that plaintiffs' demands are usually double the amount the plaintiff's lawyer believes a "best case" would produce. No plaintiff's lawyer expects her initial demand to be met; they will usually settle early in the case for perhaps 30% less.

Your hotel client wants to settle the case as soon as possible and has given you the authority to settle it for up to $1 million. But you believe that the plaintiff (like virtually all plaintiffs) will take something less than the demand.

You are familiar with the contract formation rules that a rejection terminates an offer and that a counteroffer is both a rejection and a new offer. You want to get the plaintiff to settle for something less than the full amount the plaintiff's lawyer demanded, yet you want to keep the plaintiff's offer open so you can snap it up if the plaintiff's lawyer shows any evidence that she knows more than she seems to.

Task One:

The usual practice in our jurisdiction is to respond to a personal injury plaintiff's written demand with a telephone call. (The "usual practice" can vary both by specialty and locality and is something lawyers beginning their practice must find out in order to function competently). To make such a call, the defense lawyer has to prepare for the negotiation that might ensue. And to do that, the careful defense lawyer will write out the points she wants to cover in the negotiation and, where exact language is important, write out the exact language in order to minimize error. While the plaintiff's lawyer may not take the call since she wants to catch YOU by surprise, rather than the other way around, you need to prepare as if she will.

Your talking points would normally include your alternative version of the plaintiff's damage claims (e.g., "Your client's PTSD is bull and the jury will know that"), all the reasons why the plaintiff will not be able to prove liability (e.g., "our experts will testify that we have the best security in the business"), the time and expense it will take the plaintiff's lawyer to try the case, the problems this will present to the plaintiff, and so on. Eventually, you will get around to stating the amount of money YOU think should settle the case. You figure that an opening number of $450,000 — which you describe as "generous" — is the way to start.

Your primary objective during this phone call is to keep the plaintiff's settlement offer open while still negotiating with the plaintiff over the amount that should settle the case. Focus on that part of your talking points; what language will you use to accomplish this? After you have written your answer, consult Self-Assessment 1 for Exercise D on the LexisNexis web course. In that Self-Assessment, we have given you examples of how several defense lawyers would have handled this kind of problem.

If this case settles in its current posture, following your phone call and a confirming letter, how legally durable will the resulting settlement agreement be? Is a lawyer permitted to snap up a settlement offer that may well be based on the other side's incomplete knowledge?

Imagine success in settling this case for $600,000. Your client would, justifiably, be elated that you had, on paper, saved the client $400,000. But suppose that after the money had been paid and papers signed, the plaintiff's lawyer found out about the key "side business" and sought rescission. Will this settlement contract hold up? To back it up one step, are there limits on a lawyer's concluding, on behalf of the client, a settlement agreement that may be based on the other side's incomplete knowledge of the case?

A good defense lawyer will think these issues through before even beginning the strategy described above.

You knew about the key manufacturing "side business" and the likely effect that evidence of it would have had on the jury. While you would undoubtedly fight its admissibility, the evidence is likely relevant, admissible, and *very* prejudicial. There was no suggestion in the demand letter that the plaintiff's lawyer was aware of the key operation. Indeed, the hotel wanted to settle fast precisely because it thought that the plaintiff was unaware of the key "side business".

We want to briefly explore here the legal and ethical implications of forming a contract with the plaintiff under these circumstances.

Most defense clients would not want to form a settlement contract that is avoidable by the plaintiff. That would give the plaintiff the option to keep the money or avoid the settlement and go to trial. A lawyer that exposed her client to such a risk without the client's full participation could be liable to the client for malpractice if a loss resulted. But even if the client wanted to run the risk of a rescission claim, the lawyer may be limited by professional conduct rules in what she can do even if the client were to demand it.

Professional Limitations in Negotiations

It is easiest to begin with the limits imposed on lawyers as professionals. Model Rule of Professional Conduct 1.2(d) provides:

> A lawyer shall not counsel a client to engage, or assist a client, in conduct that the lawyer knows is criminal or fraudulent. . . .

"Fraudulent," according to commentary,

> "refer[s] to conduct that is characterized as such under the substantive or procedural law of the applicable jurisdiction and has a purpose to deceive. This does not include merely negligent misrepresentation or negligent failure to apprise another of relevant information."

Model Rule of Professional Conduct 1.0, Comment 5.

It is an early lesson in Professional Responsibility that the lawyer is an independent professional who is answerable to a community other than the clients. "The client told me to do it" will not be a defense in a proceeding for professional sanctions, such as suspension from law practice, if the lawyer has run afoul of the professional responsibility rules that limit what a lawyer can do. An early article on this subject made a corollary of this basic point in a way that is helpful in our context:

If he is a professional and not merely a hired . . . hand, the lawyer is not free to do anything his client might do in the same circumstances. The corollary of that proposition does set a minimum standard: the lawyer must be at least as candid and honest as his client would be required to be. The agent of the client, that is, his attorney-at-law, must not perpetrate the kind of fraud or deception that would vitiate a bargain if practiced by his principal.[2]

This all means that, as a matter of professional ethics, the lawyer cannot perpetrate or participate in the client's fraud even if the client is willing to run the risk.

Since the law governing lawyers will follow general law on this question, the inquiry here becomes whether the law generally will require disclosure in the circumstances of our problem. If generally-applicable law does not require disclosure, then we can both proceed ethically under the professional responsibility rules and be reasonably confident that the resulting agreement will not likely be subject to rescission under contract law on account of the omitted facts.[3]

Contract Law Constraints in Negotiations

You probably knew before you came to law school that one is not permitted to misstate material facts in connection with the making of a contract. To do so would be to trick the other side; in law, this goes by the names "misrepresentation" or "fraud." Contract law provides that such a contract will be avoidable for misrepresentation, and tort law may well give the opponent a cause of action *in tort* for fraud. As suggested above, a lawyer's knowing involvement in a client's misrepresentation can expose the lawyer to sanctions for professional misconduct. It can also expose the lawyer to civil liability as a participant.[4]

Non-disclosure, or silence, about known facts is a different matter, however. Here, the law is extremely complicated and context-sensitive. Part of what makes this a far more difficult inquiry is our cultural context. In the United States, we place a great deal of responsibility for mistakes on the individuals who make them.

---

[2] Alvin B. Rubin, *A Causerie on Lawyer's Ethics in Negotiations*, 35 LA. L. REV. 577, 589 (1975) *quoted in* Nathan Crystal, *The Lawyer's Duty To Disclose Material Facts In Contract Or Settlement Negotiations*, 87 KY. L.J. 1055, 1068-69 (1999).

[3] **Sidebar: Non-disclosure converted into affirmative misrepresentation**
The negotiation in this case will probably have to be very carefully thought out so the negotiator will not be trapped into making what will later be characterized as a misrepresentation. So, for example, if the plaintiff's lawyer asks "is there some big smoking gun I don't know about?" you could be in danger of a misrepresentation challenge if your answer were "no." Part of your preparation for the negotiation will entail anticipating "trap" questions such as that and figuring out a way to address them. Answering, "that's what discovery is for" to the question above would probably be an innocuous answer. These questions tend to be generic and once you have thought out how to approach them, that learning will become part of the reservoir of your experience to pass on to others.

[4] *E.g.* Cresswell v. Sullivan & Cromwell, 668 F. Supp. 166 (S.D.N. Y. 1987), *aff'd in part vacated in part*, 922 F. 2d 60 (2d Cir. 1990).

There are many cases and a substantial literature on "disclosure" in different contexts. Statutes require, for example, that sellers of securities "disclose" relevant information to prospective investors. Lawyers have obligations to disclose facts that might impair their full representation of a client such as self-interest or conflicts of interest. With some narrow exceptions,[5] the Restatement of Contracts (Second) approaches the subject not as a duty to disclose problem but as a "relief from mistake" problem. Two provisions that are relevant here provide:

§ 153. When Mistake of One Party Makes a Contract Voidable

Where a mistake of one party at the time a contract was made as to a basic assumption on which he made the contract has a material effect on the agreed exchange of performances that is adverse to him, the contract is voidable by him if he does not bear the risk of the mistake under the rule stated in § 154, and

. . . .

(b) the other party had reason to know of the mistake or his fault caused the mistake.

§ 154. When a Party Bears the Risk of a Mistake

A party bears the risk of a mistake when

. . . .

(b) he is aware, at the time the contract is made, that he has only limited knowledge with respect to the facts to which the mistake relates but treats his limited knowledge as sufficient

Task Two:

When a problem worries you enough to do some research, it is a good practice to memorialize the research and what you concluded in a memo or notes to the file. As you develop your skills in your practice, creating these memos becomes the job of summer or junior associates.

Carefully reread the letter from the plaintiff's lawyer and assume that you wanted to form a settlement agreement for $600,000 without revealing anything about the key "side business" that you and your client correctly perceived would be so devastating to your case. Write a short (2 or 3 paragraphs) memo to the file on whether, *under the Restatement provisions above,* the resulting settlement contract would be avoidable by the plaintiff because you knew about the key "side business" but did not reveal it in your negotiations with the plaintiff's lawyer. After you have written your answer, consult Self-Assessment 2 for Exercise D on the LexisNexis web course to assess your answer.

---

[5] The Restatement (Second) of Contracts, § 161, addresses situations in which non-disclosure may be treated as an "assertion" thereby giving rise to an action for misrepresentation. It is narrowly drawn; suffice it to say that none of the instances stated in that provision will apply here.

Chapter 5
DRAFTING A CONTRACT FROM A FORM

PREVIEW

In this exercise, you will draft a simple non-commercial contract of sale for a client. It is unusual (but not unheard of) for a lawyer to become involved in a situation like the one we confront here. We have used a simple example to make this kind of drafting easier to understand for those just beginning or in the middle of their law school career.

SUBSTANTIVE CONTENT:

- UCC § 2-201 Statute of Frauds
- UCC § 2-314 Warranty of Merchantability
- UCC § 2-316(3)(a) "As is" disclaimer of warranties
- Revised UCC § 1-301 Choice of Law

SKILLS AND VALUES UTILIZED:

- Thinking through what the client's contract will require after understanding the client's situation.
- Finding form contracts on Lexis.
- Using a form as a check-list for what to include in a simple sales contract.
- Drafting a simple sales contract.

ESTIMATED TIME FOR COMPLETION: 75 Minutes

LEVEL OF DIFFICULTY (1 to 5):

Contracts and Writings:

In many settings, including those like the one hypothesized in this Chapter, people might accomplish their exchange (something of value in exchange for money) without using any writing at all. You have probably sold something to someone else, face-to-face, by simply trading the good for the money. Most would probably be surprised that even this simple exchange was a *contract*, though in most cases that fact will have little significance. Perhaps they even would be more surprised to learn that it was a contract covered by the Uniform Commercial Code (UCC). None of this matters very much in casual sales because extremely few of them ever result in a legal problem.

The UCC requires that contracts for sale in excess of $500[1] be memorialized through a writing. This requirement is commonly called the Statute of Frauds.[2] But the writing requirement only becomes relevant *after* the contract is made and *before* the exchange actually happens, that is, only when there is a gap between the making of the contract and the physical exchange of goods for money. In most of the casual "sales cases" in our personal experience, the contract is made and performed at the same time, so the writing requirement comes and goes as quickly as the contract.

Where what is exchanged is worth more than $500, the UCC requires a writing.[3] The writing requirement does not necessarily need or require a lawyer's involvement. In casual sales settings, if either party thinks they need a writing, one or the other might simply take a stab at it: non-lawyers can write perfectly acceptable sales contracts. Once in a while, a lawyer will be brought in to do the drafting.

Using Contract Forms for Drafting Contracts:

Few lawyers will draft any contract from scratch. Rather, they will consult an analogous contract that they or someone they know has drafted in the past, will buy a form from a legal stationary supplier, which is common in real estate,[4] or will consult a "form book." Form books are available in hard copy in any law library and, increasingly, in electronic form through services like Lexis. In this exercise, you will use Lexis.com to help you with your drafting.

---

[1] At least one state has increased this amount. *See., e.g., M.C.L.A. § 440.2201(2002) (Michigan increased the amount to $1,000 before requiring a contract for the sale of goods to be written.)*

[2] UCC § 2-201. You might be further surprised to learn that this writing requirement is very controversial (it was almost deleted in the latest UCC drafting effort) and has many exceptions to escape its technical rigor.

[3] Sellers and buyers unaware of the requirement may simply not comply, accomplish their sale, and move on. If the sale breaks down before performance and the parties do not simply walk away, there may be litigation. But even if there is, one of many exceptions could well nullify the requirement. As indicated above, if there is trouble after the physical exchange is made, the Statute of Frauds will have no applicability.

[4] For on-line examples, go to http://www.blumberg.com/invoice.cgi?rm=view_cluster;cluster_id=1460694.

No form will fit a given situation perfectly. Because many commercial forms are designed to be useful in a wide variety of settings, they have a great deal in them that is not usable at all for the task at hand. Those who make the best use of off-the-shelf forms will use them primarily as check lists for what might be included in their unique contract; they will never use any part of them without first ensuring that the clause in question fits the facts at hand and without understanding every word that will be used.

Drafting anything — a contract, a pleading, a discovery request, a motion, a brief, etc. — is hardest the first time. It is important for that first effort to be as good as it can be because it likely will form a template for future drafts of the same kind of document. Indeed, many lawyers have *their own* form books, full of documents *they* have drafted, to make subsequent efforts go that much more easily. Obviously, you do not want a less-than-best first effort replicating itself over and over during the course of your career.

So, while almost everyone will use a form book or someone else's old contract for guidance in drafting their own contract, good lawyers become that way by adding their own professional judgment and language, thereby improving on what came before. There is nothing memorable, or good, about a lawyer-drafted contract that is simply a cut and paste of form book language. There is craftsmanship to drafting: the voice, clarity, and, indeed, effectiveness of drafted contracts are unique to the persons who draft them.

This Chapter will proceed in three parts. First, after understanding the client's goals, you will think through what his contract may require. Second, after consulting as "check lists" a form and your own thinking from Step 1, you will list questions that you need answered by the client in order to draft what he wants. Third, using the form as *very loose* guidance, you will draft the contract.

EXERCISE E

Jack Johannsen is a long-standing client for whom you've worked for many years as his personal lawyer. He is also a technology nut, one that simply *must* have the latest of everything. Jack has just purchased a *very* high end personal computer that cost him $6,0000. Now he wants to sell his old one, a perfectly-good, six month old Giga 7500 worth about $3000, used. With new personal computers selling for under $500, there is a fairly narrow market for used machines at this value. Jack has advertised and found a buyer, Evangeline Scott, who will pay $2,800 for it. Once he has a firm buyer, it will take Jack about a week to have the hard drives cleansed of his data so no hacker can get at it, but he does not want to spend the money to do this until he has a buyer that is contractually committed. With the Giga depreciating by the day, Jack needs a very quick turnaround.

Task One:

It is very useful and good practice to simply *think* about what the client's contract will require before you begin to consult others' ideas. Form drafters are not omniscient and may not see things that are unique to your particular situation. This step permits you to bring *your* training and knowledge to bear on the particulars.

Make a list of the elements or items that you think should be reflected in the sales contract you are going to prepare. After you have written your answer, consult Self-Assessment 1 for Exercise E on the LexisNexis web course.

Task Two:

Now that you have thought about what the contract requires, you can consult a form to see if there are things you might have left out. In some respects, this is like identifying the "issues" that might be present in a simple sale of goods and deciding whether to deal with them in the writing.[5]

Go to **Lexis.com > Transactional Advisor > Commercial > Create and Draft Documents > Sales and Vendor Agreements - Sale of Goods (Article 2) > Basic Agreement for Sale of Goods**.

Read the form and then create from it a list of questions for Jack that will enable you to draft his contract. Make a separate list of any legal questions you need answers to in order to draft well. After you have written your answer, consult Self-Assessment 2 for Exercise D on the LexisNexis web course.

Some in's and out's of sales under UCC Article 2:

As you read through the form, you could see that it was drafted for a far bigger, multiple-delivery and payment situation very unlike our own. That form was a full-fledged commercial contract. This dissonance might prompt us to find a simpler form but let's continue to work with this one.

There is a great deal in this complex form that we do not need. The sales tax provision would have required you to visit the library or ask a colleague if sales taxes were due on casual sales and, if so, how they get paid. In some states, casual sales of automobiles trigger sales tax obligations. But since cars have Certificates of Title that the State has to process in order to alter ownership, the state can bill the new buyer for

---

[5] In some cases, parties aware of given issues might elect not to deal with them in the contract because doing so might yield a negotiation impasse and kill the deal. The decision not to address a given issue depends on the likelihood it will come up, how it will affect the eventual exchange if it does, and how it will affect the making of the contract if it is put on the table for negotiation. The decision not to broach an issue that you have identified is the client's, not the lawyer's.

the sales tax. Let's assume that there is no sales tax on casual, non-automobile sales in our State.

When you study the UCC in more detail, you will learn that certain implied warranties accompany sales of goods unless they are disclaimed.[6] Only merchants who sell goods of the same kind make implied warranties of merchantability[7] but anyone can make an implied warranty of fitness for a particular purpose. Further any seller may give an express warranty. It is probably best for a seller, even in casual sales contracts, to disclaim "all warranties" and perhaps even to sell the items "as is" which has the effect of disclaiming all warranties.[8] One should confirm the disclaimer of all warranties with the client to ensure the client-seller did not actually want to give a warranty with the sale.

As to selection of a state law, for now it is sufficient for you to know that the parties can select a state's law provided there is some connection between the law they select and either them or their contract.[9] In most casual contracts between individuals, the applicable law will be that of the state where they perform their contract and, if it's a face-to-face exchange, it's easy. If the goods will travel across state lines in the delivery process, then it is probably best to pick one state's law or the other to eliminate disputes about this later. In big contracts, the subtle differences in different states' laws will matter. We can assume they will not matter here.

Task Three:

Jack has given you the following in response to your questions:

1. It's a "late Year -2 Giga 7500 Super Personal Computer."

2. The buyer will pick it up in one week at Jack's house, 2020 Canary Street, Anytown, Nostate.

3. The sale is for cash or certified or cashiers' check.

4. Sales taxes are irrelevant in this setting.

---

[6] **Sidebar:** Although warranty law is somewhat complicated, it is accurate to state that contracts governed by the UCC may contain three different warranties regarding the quality of the goods. UCC § 2-313 provides that a seller will create an express warranty pertaining to the goods if the seller states a fact or promise about the goods that becomes part of the basis of the bargain. UCC § 2-314 creates an implied warranty of merchantability for every good sold by a merchant who sells goods of that kind. And UCC § 2-315 gives an implied warranty of fitness for a particular purpose if a seller "has reason to know any particular purpose for which the goods are required and that the buyer is relying on the seller's skill or judgment to select or furnish suitable goods . . . ." The UCC also provides a mechanism that allows a seller to disclaim all implied warranties in a contract. Although there are a number of different ways to disclaim implied warranties, one of the most common is the use of the terms "as is" or "with all faults." A term that informs the buyer that the seller is disclaiming all of the possible implied warranties for a good, including "merchantability" if it is a merchant seller, generally will eliminate any possible implied warranties unless federal law prohibits such a disclaimer.

[7] UCC § 2-314.

[8] *Compare* UCC § 2-316(3)(a).

[9] UCC § 1-301 (updated version that is now the same in substance as former UCC § 1-105).

5. and 6.   Jack and buyer have agreed that the buyer can test the computer and cancel the sale that day if the sale does not meet buyer's expectations but, otherwise computer will be sold "as is." (Jack trusts that if she comes all the way to his place to get the computer, she'll love the computer and won't cancel the sale unless something is really wrong with the computer).

7. and 8.   We don't need insolvency or war clauses either way.

9. Jack doesn't know what he or the buyer would "claim" so he doesn't need any notice periods for making claims.

10. Evangeline Scott, 452 N. East Street, Anyplace, Nostate.

11. Since Jack and Evangeline are both in Nostate and Evangeline will get the computer in Nostate, there is little reason to fuss with a choice of law clause but we might as well put one in anyway.

Please draft Jack's contract for him using the form, *your own plain English*, and the specifics Jack has given you. Please be sensitive to the fact that this is a relatively small contract and that the writing should be of a size and formality to match the deal. You don't want to scare away the buyer! After you have written your answer, consult Self-Assessment 3 for Exercise D on the LexisNexis web course.

Chapter 6

PERFORMANCE AND BREACH I: HELPING A CLIENT WITH A TROUBLED CONTRACT

PREVIEW

As you have probably learned, nearly all contracts are performed voluntarily, without any need for litigation. But your own personal experience no doubt tells you that some contracts are not performed as smoothly as one would want. In smaller transactions, the parties usually work out their differences and move on. In larger contracts, they may call on lawyers to help out with the task.

Helping a client resolve ongoing contract problems is a far more common lawyer task than is litigating a breached contract. It not only requires an understanding of contract law principles, but a good sense of the client's particular situation, business, and needs, an understanding of the costs and prospects of the end-game of litigation, a good command of negotiation skills, and a good imagination. It also calls for a lot of educated guesswork that the lawyer must often perform under tremendous time pressure. Assisting a client in contract management is a very challenging job.

The design of this Chapter and the one that follows it should give you a taste for this particular kind of contract lawyer work. Each Chapter is independent of the other but for a better appreciation of the work and some of the underlying law, you should complete both Chapters. In this one, we will focus on gathering the facts and applying the law to the facts to come up with a diagnosis of the client's problem. In the succeeding Chapter, we will focus on ways to solve the problems we have identified.

You should find (or your Professor will assign you) a partner with whom to do this exercise as it will involve two interviews, one by your partner interviewing you (in role) and the other by you interviewing your partner (in role).

SUBSTANTIVE CONTENT:

- Model Rules of Professional Conduct 4.2, 1.5
- Breach
- Order of Contractual Performance
- UCC §§ 2-507, 2-503
- Implied Conditions

SKILLS AND VALUES UTILIZED:

- Interviewing
- Reviewing documents
- Drafting a memo
- Applying the correct law to the facts

ESTIMATED TIME FOR COMPLETION: 60 minutes (excluding interview time)

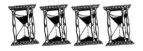

LEVEL OF DIFFICULTY (1 to 5):

EXERCISE F:

You are an Associate in your law firm. The firm wants to increase its number of pro bono hours, so it asked every associate to take on one more pro bono case. After you agreed, the firm assigned to you the case of Brenda Ware.

The file contains the following information from the pro bono coordinator:

Ms. Ware lives in an area in the Midwest recently devastated by many storms that caused horrendous flooding and destruction. She lost her home in the aftermath of the storms and floods and has been living in a trailer provided by FEMA (Federal Emergency Management Agency). Ms. Ware was fortunate enough to have had her home insured and the proceeds from the insurance enabled her to buy a new modular home to replace the home she lost in the flood.

There are no issues with the insurance company; the company paid on the policy in a timely manner. Ms. Ware's problem is with her future living arrangements. She paid a cash deposit from the insurance proceeds to YOUTrust Homes to purchase a modular home that is to be placed on her real estate. Her contact at YOUTrust is a salesman named Carl Spokes. The problem presented in the file is that she has been told that she must vacate her FEMA trailer in the very near future and the home has not been delivered. She has nowhere else to live. YOUTrust is demanding the balance of the purchase price before they will deliver the home and Ms. Ware is afraid to pay them, unless she knows she definitely will have her home delivered in a timely manner.

You need to interview her to gather the details of her case. The file also contained a copy of the signed agreement between YOUTrust and Ms. Ware (set out below) and the following picture of Mrs. Ware's favorite restaurant as it looks today. She put it into the file so those working with the case would get a better idea of what happened.

PURCHASE AGREEMENT
5678 BRIDGE St, Rapidville, IA 54321 •
123 – 456 – 1234 Fax 123 – 456 – 5678

Purchaser(s): Brenda Ware   Phone: 515-555-1212   Date: 10-05-00

Address: 123 Main Street   City: Rivertown   State: IA   ZIP: 70055   Cty: St. Stevens

Subject to the terms on reverse side, the purchaser agrees to purchase the following home for the price set forth:

New Used	Size: **1200 s.f.**	Color: **Blue**	Stock#:	Year: **0000**
Make:	Trade Name:		Model #: L6789012	
Serial #:Special Order			Cash Selling Price	$100,000

[Delivery, Blocking, Anchoring and Leveling to Manufacturer's and State Specifications]				
1. Air Conditioning Y/N		1. Land Purchase	$	
2. Refrigerator Y/N	$	2. Clean Site/Demolition	$	
3. Elec. Stove Y/N	$	3. Foundation	$ **Inc.**	
4. Microwave Y/N	$	4. Electrical Services	$ **Inc.**	
5. Dishwasher Y/N	$	5. Water or Well Install	$ **Inc.**	
6. Disposal Y/N	$	6. Sewer Install	$ **Inc.**	
7. Washer Y/N	$	7. Deck or Patio Install	$	
8. Dryer Y/N	$	8. Drive or Walk Install	$	
9: Other: _____	$	9. Carport/Garage Install	$	
10: Other: _____		10: Other: _____	$	
Sub – Total:	$	**Sub – Total:**	$	

Setup and Finish			**Sub – Totals Carried**	**$100,000**
1. Steps (Wood)	Yes No		**Total Price**	**$100,000**
2. Steps (Cement)	Yes No	**Insurance Agent**	Plus Sales Tax _____%	$
3. Steps (Fiberglass)	Yes No	Co:	Title Fees	$
4. Skirting Supplied	Yes No	Nm:	Miscellaneous Fees	$
5. Skirting Installed	Yes No	Phn:	Insurance	$
6. Other: _____	Yes No	Fax:	**Sub – Total**	**$100,000**
7. Other: _____	Yes No		Deposit	**$50,000**
		Trade Allowance	$	
		Trade Payoff	$	
			Net Trade	$
			Total Unpaid Balance	**$50,000**

Other Items to Include or Removed: Trade		**Trade Description, If Applicable**		
		Make/Year:	Trade Name:	
		Model #:	Color: Size:	
Estimated Term of Loan: ____ mnths/$ ____ pmt		Serial #:	Payoff To:	

**NOTE: The undersigned purchaser's agree that the deposit paid for the purchase of the home will be forfeited/no-refundable in the event the sale is not consummated or completed through no fault of seller. Initial _____

Brenda Ware 10/17/0000		0000842	012-34-5678
Purchaser's Signature	Date	Driver's License #	Social Security #

Purchaser's Signature	Date	Driver's License #	Social Security #

Carl Spokes 10/17/00			
YOUTrust Homes, L.L.C. - Seller		Date *10/17/0000*	Salesperson *Carl Spokes*

TERMS

The purchase of the subject mobile home, as described herein below, shall be pursuant to the following terms:

a. YOUTrust Homes, L.L.C. agrees to deliver, block, anchor and level the home to manufacturer's specifications and state codes. Please Note: This work is subcontracted out by YOUTrust Homes, L.L.C.

b. A manufacturer's warranty [ ] does [ ] does not come with this home, the terms of which are found in the Owner's Manual to be provided by the manufacturer with the delivery of the home, NOTE: All warranties are provided by Manufacturer and NOT by YOUTrust Homes, L.L.C.[1]

c. There is a limited day cosmetic warranty - see Owner's Manual for details.

d. YOUTrust Homes, L.L.C. and any contractors of YOUTrust Homes, L.L.C. do not re-level mobile homes after the initial setup without charging a fee. Re-leveling is needed periodically and is not included in the cost of the home.

e. Neither YOUTrust Homes, L.L.C. nor their contractors are responsible for the hook-up of any utilities, nor do they provide any supplies or labor for utility hook-ups.

---

[1] Authors' Note: Note that under Terms (b) no box was checked. From YOUTrust's perspective that was not a good move because, if it did not intend to give a manufacturer's warranty, it should clearly indicate that under the terms. The Uniform Commercial Code supplies "implied warranties" in many sales of goods cases *unless* the seller disclaims them. In addition, Ms. Ware did not initial the language at the end. Were a dispute to arise about who was to prepare the site, this uninitialed provision might well throw the responsibility on the drafter / seller.

  It is not unusual for lawyers to draft documents for clients and then have the clients fail to use them correctly. Training clients how to use form correctly is just as important as drafting excellent documents for their use. A great form does no good if it is not used properly.

The purchaser is responsible for site preparation and complying with all other provisions of la. R. S. 51:912.22 with regard to site preparation (i.e., clearing and leveling land, etc.). Initial_____

Task One:

Your first task is to travel to the area and interview Ms. Ware to determine the extent of her legal problem and how you can assist her. Thus, you are on a fact-finding mission. Your partner will play the role of Ms. Ware and will have a script. You should both assume roles of lawyer and flood-victim-client. Your job is to establish a rapport with your client and obtain all of the relevant facts to help resolve her problem. The student who is role playing Ms. Ware should obtain the Ware facts from the LexisNexis web course.

To get the most out of this exercise, you should both take the role play seriously and stay in role. It should not take more than 20–30 minutes to get the information from your role-playing partner. Once you have completed your interview and have your notes consult Self-Assessment 1 for Exercise F on the LexisNexis web course.

Now that you have the facts from your client's point of view and a copy of the contract, what should be your next steps? Stop here and list them and prioritize them. Once you have done so, read on.

[THIS PAGE IS INTENTIONALLY LEFT BLANK]

What is the next logical step? Your list might have included "write YOUTrust a letter or call YOUTrust." In some settings a letter would be a good way to proceed: you could carefully choose your language, and you would have a record of exactly what you wrote. The problem is that a letter (or e-mail) will trigger a similarly calculated response from the other side and that carefully crafted response may not tell you much that is useful about YOUTrust's real position. More important, because of what you have learned from Ms. Ware, moving quickly is very important.

Is there any reason not to call YOUTrust?

One major reason not to call would be if Carl Spokes or YOUTrust were represented by counsel. Model Rule of Professional Conduct 4.2 provides limits on communications with those represented by counsel. It provides:

> In representing a client, a lawyer shall not communicate about the subject of the representation with a person the lawyer knows to be represented by another lawyer in the matter, unless the lawyer has the consent of the other lawyer or is authorized by law to do so.

Spokes may not *be* YOUTrust Homes but, as an employee, he would likely be covered by this prohibition if you knew YOUTrust to be represented.

Assume that YOUTrust has no attorney that you know of, so there is no reason not to contact Mr. Spokes at YOUTrust and see whether you can work to resolve the problems without going to court. This is certainly the best option for your client.

Task Two:

It is time to get the story from the other side. While in real life you might be able to interview Mr. Spokes by telephoning him, here you will interview him in person.

Now switch places with your interviewing partner: former Ms. Ware should interview YOUTrust's Carl Spokes and get his side of the story. The student who is role playing Mr. Spokes should obtain the Spokes facts from the LexisNexis web course.

Again, to get the most out of this exercise, please take it seriously and stay in role. It should not take more than 20–30 minutes to get the information from him.

Once you have completed your interview and have your notes consult Self-Assessment 2 for Exercise F on the LexisNexis web course.

Task Three:

It is now time for a preliminary diagnosis. Review your notes on your two interviews and re-read the contract between Ms. Ware and

YOUTrust thoroughly. Be sure to highlight any contract provisions that you think may be important in resolving the problem.

For purposes here, we can assume that the contract is valid (despite the many blanks in it), that it is supported by consideration, and that it was entered into by both parties in good faith. What problem do we confront with moving this contract forward and how do you think we should try to resolve that problem? Remembering that litigation is expensive and that nearly all disputes are settled without it, litigation may not be the first choice in how to proceed. What steps do you need to take, before litigation. Jot down your answers.

After you have written your answer, consult Self-Assessment 3 for Exercise F on the LexisNexis web course. Then proceed to the following pages.

The Law's Role in this Impasse: Order of Contractual Performance

Despite the fact that the contract is stuck and you simply want to get it unstuck, the law has an indirect, but important, role to play in the upcoming negotiation. It is therefore very important to understand the legal setting in which the parties find themselves. It is also important to realize, even at this stage in your legal education, that the rules of contract law play only a part in the overall solution to a contract problem.

The law usually saddles one side or the other with liability for breach. So who is, or will be, in breach if things remain unchanged? Review the facts: your client refuses to pay the remaining money owed on the contract until she gets what she contracted for, and the seller will not deliver the goods without first receiving the money owed on the contract. We have a classic problem involving the order in which performances are to take place. In many settings, someone *has* to perform (or begin performing) first.

A simple example will suffice. If this were a case where a child were trading a doll for a stuffed animal and did not trust her trading partner, you could imagine each putting their hands on the other's toy and creating a simultaneous exchange. But simultaneous exchange is not possible in most kinds of contracts. An hourly worker is not dispensed cash minute-by-minute as she works; she is paid at the end of the week or the month. She works first, *then* she gets paid. Lawyers, by taking retainers, reverse this order — they get money *first* and then they do the work.[2] The same generally holds true for landlords and many utility companies that require advance deposits from their customers. Since each party to a contract usually has to do or pay something, the recurring question in all kinds of contracts is "who has to perform first." As you can imagine, contract law has rules to address this ever-present problem in contract performance. We are fortunate that Article 2 of the UCC, the statute that will govern this transaction,[3] supplies some statutory rules to help reach a resolution.

In this case, the timing question is: does Ms. Ware have to pay *before* the seller delivers and installs the house, or does YOUTrust have to deliver the house to her property *before* she has to pay? Consider the following relevant excerpts from the UCC.

---

[2] The text is not strictly accurate. A lawyer's retainer is an advance against fees that will be incurred — it is like a deposit and is typically taken for security in payment. Model Rule of Professional Conduct 1.5 requires that "A lawyer's fee shall be reasonable." Comment 2 says "A lawyer may require advance payment of a fee, but is obliged to return any unearned portion."

[3] It is not self evident that the sale of a "modular home" is a "sale of goods" thereby coming under the provisions of Article 2 of the Uniform Commercial Code. In real life, one would research the question of what law applies since the applicable rules might differ depending on the answer. The earlier chapter, Introduction to Choice of Law and the Scope of the UCC develops this part of this problem.

§ 2-507. Effect of Seller's Tender; Delivery on Condition.

(1) Tender of delivery is a condition to the buyer's duty to accept the goods and, unless otherwise agreed, to his duty to pay for them. Tender entitles the seller to acceptance of the goods and to payment according to the contract.

§ 2-503. Manner of Seller's Tender of Delivery.

(1) Tender of delivery requires that the seller put and hold conforming goods at the buyer's disposition and give the buyer any notification reasonably necessary to enable him to take delivery. The manner, time and place for tender are determined by the agreement and this Article, and in particular

(a) tender must be at a reasonable hour, and if it is of goods they must be kept available for the period reasonably necessary to enable the buyer to take possession; but

(b) unless otherwise agreed the buyer must furnish facilities reasonably suited to the receipt of the goods.

Task Four

Now, consider the sales contract. Where is language within that contract that speaks to our timing question? After reviewing the provisions above (hard to understand as they might be) and the language of the contract, write a memo (no more than one page) as to which party, if this impasse continues, is most likely in breach for not paying or for not delivering. Be sure to use the UCC sections listed above and the contract language when writing your memo.

Consult Self-Assessment 4 for Exercise D on the LexisNexis web course.

It is important to recognize that however strong the argument that YOUTrust is in breach might be, we are not before a court — nor do we want to be. It may at some point be necessary to develop a legal argument around our legal conclusions but, in this context, assertions of legal argument may be counterproductive. The client may be legally entitled to have the home delivered before she pays, but in the real world, that may only entitle the client to recover damages through litigation that may literally take years. In the meantime, if YOUTrust refuses to comply with its legal obligations, the client will be out her $50,000 deposit (at least in the short run), have no place to live, and will have to finance what may be protracted litigation to recover her deposit or obtain her mobile home. You also will be out the time that it takes to work on this pro bono case. Therefore, the advice you give your client should be that she should allow you to try to work out a solution to move beyond this impasse.

Task Five:

Now please think about mechanisms the parties might be willing to agree to in order to move beyond the impasse and jot down your suggestions. After you have written down your suggestions, consult Self-Assessment 5 for Exercise F on LexisNexis web course.

Task Six:

Take the short review quiz on this material on the web course.

Chapter 7

PERFORMANCE AND BREACH II — RESOLVING A CONTRACT IMPASSE

PREVIEW

In this Chapter, you are representing a pro bono client, living in a FEMA trailer, who has bought a modular home but cannot get it delivered until she pays the full price. Because she distrusts the seller, she is unwilling to pay the full price until the seller delivers the home and sets it onto its foundation.

This impasse is a classic contract performance problem and clients call on lawyers to help them with such problems every day.

The central objective in nearly all such situations is to get the contract back on track and performed. Litigation, even when a client is clearly in the right, is a very poor substitute for actual performance. Consider that damages, if they are awarded and paid in this case, will arrive a long time after the problem arose and, in the meanwhile, the client may have nowhere to live. Moreover, the client will pay the lawyer's fee out of those damages. (In the United States, parties pay their own lawyers in most situations, win or lose). In contract settings, the winning post-litigation client will almost always be worse off, usually far worse off, than she would have been had the parties found a way to get the contract performed when the problems arose.

The exercises in this chapter require you to examine the litigation option and then several other solutions that might solve the client's problem. To do so, you will have to think through proposed contract clauses from the perspectives of parties who now distrust one another. In the final exercise, you will draft a contract provision that you think will permit the contract to move forward.

SUBSTANTIVE CONTENT:

- Brief overview of escrow agreements

SKILLS AND VALUES UTILIZED:

- Reviewing and analyzing complex contract language
- Techniques to help understand the other side's point of view in a contract dispute
- Redrafting

ESTIMATED TIME FOR COMPLETION: 75 Minutes

LEVEL OF DIFFICULTY (1 to 5):

EXERCISE G:

This is a continuation of the problem Performance and Breach I: Helping a Client with a Troubled Contract — involving Ms. Ware and YOUTrust Modular Homes. If you have worked with that problem, you will recall that Ms. Ware, a victim of a flood that destroyed her house, received insurance proceeds and contracted to buy a modular home from YOUTrust to be installed on her now empty real estate. The total price was $100,000; she paid $50,000 down. The home has arrived at YOUTrust's showroom but the company has demanded that Ms. Ware pay the remaining $50,000 before they deliver the home and install it on her property. Ms. Ware did not want to do that. In the meanwhile, her "home" is a FEMA trailer that smells of formaldehyde. FEMA has been pressuring her to vacate the trailer. She has no other housing options.

After interviewing Ms. Ware and a YOUTrust representative and reviewing the sales contract (it is printed in Performance and Breach I) and provisions of Article 2 of the UCC, you have determined that the applicable law requires 1) payment after delivery is made and 2) delivery of the home where the parties agree it should be delivered. From the facts, you have determined that the agreed place for delivery is Ms. Ware's real estate, not in the showroom.

This means that YOUTrust is *not* entitled to payment *before* it delivers and installs the home on Ms. Ware's real estate. Refusing delivery to the real estate unless it is paid first is a demand that YOUTrust may not make. Importantly, in the contract YOUTrust drafted, it *could* have, but did not, condition delivery to the real estate on prior payment.

Thus, Ms. Ware could regard a refusal to deliver the home without her prior payment to be a breach by YOUTrust of the sales contract. We can assume that the lawyers for both sides probably could be safe in concluding that, if this contract failed and the case were to go to litigation, Ms. Ware would have a 70% (or better) chance of prevailing on the merits.

Task One:

You are handling this case on a pro bono basis and Ms. Ware qualifies for your services because of her low income. She is the divorced mother of a teenage son and she desperately wants to move out of her FEMA trailer (remember, it has that funny formaldehyde smell) and into her new modular home. YOUTrust, on the other hand, is a fairly large organization with ready access to lawyers and undoubtedly more funds to pay for litigation than Ms. Ware. Your legal training has told you that your client has at least a 70% chance of winning a lawsuit. You also know that there is little chance of resolving this by litigation in less than a year and that the majority of disputes are resolved without litigation. You have gathered the facts and done enough research to be reasonably confident about the law.

What do you think your next steps should be? Write a paragraph describing your next steps. After you have written your answer, consult Self-Assessment 1 for Exercise G on the LexisNexis webcourse.

Figure 1:   Another flood picture that fell out of the file

New Developments

YOUTrust may have been thinking of the losses it might sustain if litigation ensues because it hired Gerry Johanssen, Esq., to represent it. Ms. Ware brought you a letter and proposed "escrow agreement" that she received from Mr. Johanssen and asked your advice on whether she should sign the agreement. The letter and Escrow Agreement are printed below.

An escrow agreement, as used in this context, is a protective device that allows the deposit of funds with a third party who releases those funds only when a certain event happens. By its nature, an Escrow Agreement is designed to release the funds held by the agent on the happening of whatever "trigger"[1] the parties agree to. It is a three-way contract: the parties define that trigger and agree to it as the condition for release of the funds; the agent agrees to release the funds only when that condition is satisfied. These arrangements are most useful when the parties do not trust one another.[2]

It is obviously critical to both of the parties that the trigger be properly defined: if it is too "loose," the money could be released before the vendor has completed its performance; if it is too tight, the vendor might not be able to get the money without litigation, even if it has fully performed.

A couple of illustrations will make this clearer. What would be wrong, for example, with a trigger that provided "Agent will release the funds when vendor makes a request to agent that it release funds," a trigger somewhat similar to the one you will see below? Obviously, the vendor might make such a request before completing its performance, thereby depriving the buyer of the leverage over the seller that anticipated payment provides. What would be wrong with a trigger that provided "Agent will release the funds when vendee certifies in writing that she is fully and completely satisfied with vendor's performance?" Obviously, the vendee might *never* be fully satisfied. Worse the vendee may realize that by denying full satisfaction she can deny payment. The vendor might then have to resort to litigation to get its payment.

Here is what Mr. Johanssen sent Ms. Ware.

---

[1] The "trigger" may be as simple as presenting a document showing that goods were delivered to a certain place on a certain date, to having a seller make some (defined) showing that it has fixed the defects in the real estate being sold.

[2] **Sidebar: The "Letter of Credit"**
A very common device used in international trade is the "Letter of Credit." These are sophisticated three-party arrangements in which a bank holds the buyer's funds until the seller presents the bank with official documents (that the parties define) showing (usually) that the seller has performed its side of the bargain. If those documents are what was agreed to, the bank will pay the seller. While governed by international standards and sometimes by statutes, they work in a way that is very similar to the simpler escrow agreements we are working with in this Chapter. Because many international traders are strangers who have little basis to trust one another, and because international litigation is prohibitively expensive, letters of credit make many international transactions possible.

Dear Ms. Ware:

Enclosed is an escrow agreement signed by my client. Kindly execute it and deposit the remaining $50,000 with Merchant Title, LLC and I will instruct my client to deliver your home and install it on your property.

This offer expires 10 days from the date of this letter.

Sincerely,

Gerry Johanssen, Esq.
Attorney for YOUTrust Homes, LLC

The Escrow Agreement to which the letter referred is reprinted verbatim below. (It was not very well-drafted. Not all lawyers are as careful or well-trained as one might wish).

ESCROW AGREEMENT

Property: 123 Main Street, Rapidville, IOWA

This Escrow Agreement (the "Agreement") made by and between Buyer Brenda Ware (hereafter referred to as "Purchaser") and YOUTrust HOMES of IOWA, LLC (hereinafter referred to as 'Vendor"), and Merchant Title, LLC, through the undersigned duly authorized agent (hereinafter referred to as "Escrow Agent").

WITNESSETH:

Purchaser and Vendor pursuant to the sale of the PROPERTY the parties hereby agree and authorize said Escrow Agent to ESCROW the amount of $50,000.00, for the purpose of placing pilings, foundation and final electrical, in a non-interest bearing account at a bank in Rapidville, IOWA without Escrow Agent being responsible for the failure or suspension of the bank.

This Agreement shall become effective as of the date hereof and shall continue in force for a period of 30 days.

Funds shall be released to YOUTRUST HOMES, LLC upon Escrow Agent's receipt of written instructions from VENDOR (YOUTRUST) in the following two disbursements:

1. 90% of the above sum shall be disbursed to YOUTRUST Homes, LLC upon the property of pilings and secure a foundation. (verified by digital photograph)[3]

---

[3] AUTHORS' NOTE: This is the exact language you received from YOUTrust. We have not introduced typos into it.

It is an unfortunate fact of life that sometimes opponents present you with gibberish. You have to learn to cope with that too. *Calling* Johanssen and referring to his draft as "gibberish" would *not* likely advance the ball!

2. The remaining 10% shall be disbursed to YOUTRUST Homes, LLC upon the final electrical hook up/installation.

After the expiration of thirty (30) days from the execution of this agreement, the Escrow Agent reserves the right to deposit the escrowed funds with a court of competent jurisdiction. In the event any controversy arises between Purchaser and Vendor and/or any third person, the Escrow Agent shall not be required to determine the results of such controversy or to act in any way, but may await the settlement of the controversy by jointly executed written instructions between the parties to the controversy or by filing a Petition for an interpleader proceeding in a court of appropriate jurisdiction and venue and depositing the funds into the registry of the court. Upon such occurrence, this Agreement is terminated and Escrow Agent has no responsibility hereunder. Further, if this Agreement terminates or expires, the Escrow Agent shall deposit the entire amount of escrowed funds into the Registry of the Court for further determination.

[Here followed language clarifying that the escrow agent had no responsibility to investigate the facts or resolve disputes, and requiring the parties to hold the agent harmless in the event of disputes between them]

THUS DONE AND SIGNED ON THE DATE SET OPPOSITE THEIR NAMES.

WITNESSES:

		BY:		
			BUYER BRENDA. WARE	DATE
		BY:		
			YOUTRUST HOMES OF IOWA, LLC Represented herein by	DATE
		BY:		
				DATE
			Print Name	

There will be no other signatures required to distribute these funds.

Initials _____

Task Two:

Locate the "triggers" and any related provisions in this agreement that may be important in resolving this dispute. Once you have done that, briefly write out the worst case scenario that you think could occur if, after your advice, Ms. Ware were to sign the agreement as written, and deposit her money with the agent. (Be imaginative — life can be very surprising!) After you have completed that, compare it to our Client Horror Story in Self-Assessment 2 for Exercise G on the LexisNexis web course.

Task Three:

After having thought about all of the possible problems with the Escrow Agreement presented to Ms. Ware, you found an Escrow Agreement for a real estate sales contract on the Web. Starting with that, you developed one for this contract. You tentatively decided that you would propose the following version of its trigger as a replacement for the one YOUTrust sent to Ms. Ware.

> Escrow Agent shall hold the amount deposited until receipt of written authorization for its deposition signed by both Buyer and Seller. If there is any dispute as to whom Escrow Agent is to deliver the amount deposited, Escrow Agent shall hold the sum until the parties' rights are finally determined in an appropriate action or proceeding or until a court orders Escrow Agent to deposit the down payment with it. If Escrow Agent does not receive a proper written authorization from Seller and Buyer, or if an action or proceeding to determine Seller's and Buyer's rights is not begun or diligently prosecuted, Escrow Agent is under no obligation to bring an action or proceeding in court to deposit the sum held, but may continue to hold the deposit.

Write brief answers to the following questions.

1) What is required to release the funds under this proposal?

2) Now put yourself in the shoes of YOUTrust's attorney. Would you tell your client to agree to this escrow agreement? Why would such an agreement be unacceptable in our setting and to whom?

3) In thinking through this problem, again write a worse case scenario that the objecting party might imagine. After doing this, consult the Vendor Horror Story Feedback, below.[4]

---

[4] The language from which the current trigger was developed is located at (http://64.233.169.104/ search?q=cache:UJpfte9Il8EJ:www.worldlawdirect.com/builddocs/ESCROW%2520AGREEMENT.rtf +escrow+agreement&hl=en&ct=clnk&cd=1&gl=us&client=firefox-a). It reads in full:

If no closing takes place under the Contract, Escrow Agent shall continue to hold the amount deposited until receipt of written authorization for its deposition signed by both Buyer and Seller. If there is any dispute as to whom Escrow Agent is to deliver the amount deposited,

The answers to your questions ought to underscore the hazards a lawyer faces in using language designed for one situation in a situation that is different without fully understanding the dynamics of the two situations.

After you have written your answer, consult Self-Assessment 3 for Exercise G on the LexisNexis web course.

Task Four:

Imagining the objections that the other side will have to a given solution is an important step in creating a solution to which both sides can agree. Please revise the triggers in the above agreement in such a way that both sides might trust their collective arrangements and move forward with the contract.[5] After you have written your answer, consult Self-Assessment 4 for Exercise G on the LexisNexis web course.

Escrow Agent shall hold the sum until the parties' rights are finally determined in an appropriate action or proceeding or until a court orders Escrow Agent to deposit the down payment with it. If Escrow Agent does not receive a proper written authorization from Seller and Buyer, or if an action or proceeding to determine Seller's and Buyer's rights is not begun or diligently prosecuted, Escrow Agent is under no obligation to bring an action or proceeding in court to deposit the sum held, but may continue to hold the deposit.

Why might the language in the text, lifted from the language above, not be appropriate for our situation? There is a lesson here: forms that may be perfectly good for one setting can be terribly inappropriate for others.

Note that, as implicit in the first sentence of the foregoing language, in a real estate sales contract, the "closing" (sometimes called "settlement") itself releases the escrow funds. We might expect that to happen 90% or more of the time. When a closing does not take place, we could expect that, in a substantial number of cases, the parties will agree to some allocation of the escrow funds and instruct the agent. Thus, we could imagine the court contingency arising in *very* few cases under this language (a contract provision that generates litigation in even a few cases is not an optimal contract clause). Moreover, in real estate contracts, the escrow agreement is entered into as a matter of course, not because of impasse and distrust. In distrust situations as we have in our Problem, you can expect the parties *not* to agree to release the funds. This means that using party agreement as a trigger is a recipe for trouble.

Taking contract language out of a context for which it was developed and dropping it into another context is not sound practice, at least where one does not understand both contexts and the differences between them.

5   In real life, the optimal trigger language will be the result of negotiation that could result from many iterations of the language. If both parties are operating in good faith, they will attempt to create language that will work without favoring either, inasmuch as both want to perform the contract and move on. You should write language you think would work without regard to whether you would offer that language, as such, in a negotiation setting. Your teacher may decide to have teams of you produce the trigger through negotiation. If that is the case, you should follow those instructions.

Chapter 8
NO-COMPETE CONTRACTS AND THE ETHICS OF DRAFTING

PREVIEW

In this Chapter, we focus substantively on no-compete contract provisions, an increasingly common feature of the employment relationship. These are extensively regulated on public policy grounds and, while jurisdictions may articulate their rules in similar language, they vary substantially on the details and the extent to which these provisions ought to be enforceable. Our goal is not to teach the law of no-compete provisions but to introduce you to them.

This substantive focus is our vehicle for examining some of the professional responsibility issues involved in drafting contracts for clients. There are obviously limits on blindly following a client's "orders" with respect to drafting. But what are they? How flexible are they? And how does a lawyer cope with a client that demands more than the lawyer can ethically deliver?

We will ask you to develop facts that you think are necessary for coming to a judgment about how to draft a no-compete provision. We will then confront you with a client who demands too much and ask you how one might respond to such a problem. The text and feedback are designed to open your eyes to the choices lawyers have in this context and to the many ways a lawyer might respond to a difficult client.

SUBSTANTIVE CONTENT:

- Restatement of Contracts § 188 (ancillary restraints on competition)
- Model Rule of Professional Conduct 5.6
- Model Rule of Professional Conduct 1.2(d)

SKILLS AND VALUES UTILIZED:

- Fact development for fine-tuning a no-compete agreement so it is "reasonable."
- Confronting a client seeking to overreach through a contract.
- Ethical limitations on drafting contract provisions.

ESTIMATED TIME FOR COMPLETION: 60 Minutes

LEVEL OF DIFFICULTY (1 to 5):

EXERCISE H

You have a second appointment next week with a new client, Chris Colgate, DDS, a 52 year-old dentist working in city of 500,000 in otherwise-rural Anystate. You learned at an initial interview that Chris has been practicing dentistry for about 25 years and has built up what most would regard as a good practice. She works a total of 5 days a week; she is off on Wednesday afternoons and Fridays, and works Saturdays and Thursday evenings. Her annual income appears to be about $300,000 (you did not ask). While she still has at least 10 years of practice left in her, she is a planner and has begun to think about retirement and, also, about the substantial patient base she has built up over the years. The loyalty of these patients is valuable and Chris wants to realize the value of this goodwill at her point of retirement.

While many dentists just "sell" their practices to another dentist,[1] Chris said she was not ready to "sell" just yet and she has too high a regard for her patients to sell to "just anybody." Chris had a better idea. She wants to take in a young dental school graduate, let that person get to know the patients and gain the patients' trust and, after about three years, begin to transfer the ownership of the practice to the new dentist over the remaining seven years. This will allow Chris to ease off and play more golf in the near term. Perhaps more important, it will allow Chris to decide during the first few years if the new dentist can be trusted with her patients. If the new dentist is suitable, eventually she will be able to get a higher price for her practice since the new dentist will have developed patient loyalty and therefore there will be less risk in losing patients when taking over the practice.

As you talked through Chris's plan, you suggested that she was constructing, essentially a "probationary period" approaching three years for the young dentist. During that period, the newcomer is expected to develop trust with Chris's patients as well as bringing in his or her own patients.

---

[1] One place where dentists place ads to sell their dental practices is http://www.dentalsales.com/Public/PracticesForsale.aspx.

This trust, while desirable, also was a problem from Chris's perspective. The newcomer could work for a couple of years, develop patient loyalty with Chris's patients, and then quit and walk away with those patients without paying her anything. Chris would then be back to square one, but would have fewer patients. And if the newcomer was satisfactory but did not stay, Chris would have lost that much time on her plan, even if the newcomer did not "steal" patients on the way out.[2] Chris wants both to protect her patient base and to make sure a good younger dentist does not leave.

Chris has heard of "no-compete contracts"[3] and wants you to draft the key provisions for her. You told Chris that you would look into it but seemed to remember that drafting such provisions is a very complex task. You will have to get back to her.

To simplify matters, here is what *your* Summer intern brought you after you sent her on a one-hour excursion to get you some background.

[date]

To: YOU

From: Summer Intern

Re: One Hour's Research on No-Compete Contracts

You've asked me to spend an hour getting the ground rules for no compete contracts. You've told me that the client is a dentist and she wants us to draft a no compete provision for a contract with

---

[2] The newcomer runs substantial risk in this arrangement too. Unless the pay is reasonable, the new dentist might be "out of the big money" if things did not work out with Chris. If the newcomer's relationship with the practice dissolved after a period of nearly three years then he or she would have to, essentially, start over with someone new.

[3] **Sidebar on Policy Considerations behind No-compete Provisions**

Part of the problem with no compete provisions is that conditioning an individual's employment on an agreement to limit future livelihood can be seen as predatory. Our country has a long history of abusing workers, a history that started with slavery and indentured servitude, and courts have developed a tendency to favor the underdog. Except perhaps in the setting of the financial services CEO, the underdog is usually the employee. Moreover, no-compete contracts are, by definition, anti-competitive. In a staunchly capitalist culture such as ours that touts competition as a central value, courts will look askance on agreements that limit competition.

As with most questions that bring on lawyers, there is another side to the no-compete story. From an economic perspective, enforceable no-compete contracts can facilitate productive relationships that otherwise might not be possible. Chris's plan might be a case in point: if a dentist with her plan could not keep a junior partner from "stealing" the patients, she might not proceed with such a plan at all. She might, instead, sell outright. Chris's plan, on the other hand, is arguably better for Chris, the new dentist, and the patients themselves.

State law differs widely on the underlying questions and you would, no doubt, determine first what state law will or should apply to the no-compete provision and research that law.

As a draftsperson, you would inevitably put a choice of law provision (e.g., "the law of New York applies to all aspects of this contract.") into the contract in an effort to reduce uncertainty as to which law will apply. For complicated reasons, such provisions are not foolproof in this particular context. If you're *very* curious, see *Cherry, Bekaert & Holland v. Brown*, 582 So. 2d 502 (Ala. 1991) (court refused to enforce a choice of law provision in a no-compete case for public policy reasons). Depending on what is at risk and how far the client wants you to go, you might therefore go further here in trying to understand the law that might apply to the agreement. One way to better assess the legal risks and constraints is to research the law of all jurisdictions that could possibly be implicated and gear your advice to the worst-case scenario. Such research may be too expensive to be plausible in a project such as this.

a younger dentist. You said that my informal notes were all right. Here are notes on my research.

1. The Restatement (Second) of Contracts § 188 speaks to the problem. It provides, in part:

§ 188 Ancillary Restraints on Competition

(1) A promise to refrain from competition that imposes a restraint that is ancillary to an otherwise valid transaction or relationship is unreasonably in restraint of trade if

(a) the restraint is greater than is needed to protect the promisee's legitimate interest, or

(b) the promisee's need is outweighed by the hardship to the promisor and the likely injury to the public.

Subsection (2)(b) confirms that no-compete provisions made by an employee to an employer are among the situations addressed by the provision.

2. In addition to the Restatement provision, my quick review of the cases on Lexis located a case where the Arizona Supreme Court rejected a no-compete provision in a physician context in *Valley Medical Specialists v. Farber*, 982 P.2d 1277 (Ariz. 1999). The court found that not limiting the restriction to the doctor's specialty (pulmonologist), the excessive length of time (2 years) and the excessive geographical restriction (5 miles from any of 3 branch offices) took the provision out of the narrow protection offered by the law.

3. I think it was also significant to the Arizona court that this was a *physician* because the court made a point that his patients had an important interest in being able to see the doctor of their choice. The court refused to find that *all* restrictions in the doctor-patient area were void but it seemed to come close.

4. And the court made reference to the analogous case for lawyers where such restrictions *are* simply void. While this isn't directly on point, it's a point worth knowing for both of us, so I quote a provision from the Model Rules of Professional Conduct below.

Rule 5.6. Restrictions on Right to Practice

A lawyer shall not participate in offering or making:

(a) a partnership, shareholders, operating, employment, or other similar type of agreement that restricts the right of a lawyer to practice after termination of the relationship, except an agreement concerning benefits upon retirement or an agreement for the sale of a law practice consistent with Rule 1.17[4]; or

---

[4] A requirement in the sale of a law practice under referenced Rule 1.17 is that "The seller ceases to engage in private practice of law."

(b) an agreement in which a restriction on the lawyer's right to practice is part of the settlement of a controversy between private parties.[5]

Task One:

You expect Chris back next week. Having read the Summer clerk's memo, what fact questions do you need to ask Chris to get a sense for how to draft the no-compete provision? Write down the questions and after you have written your answer, consult Self-Assessment 1 for Exercise H on the LexisNexis web course.

You have concluded, under the applicable law and the facts as Chris has conveyed them, that the following no-compete provision has a good chance of being construed as "reasonable," if necessary, by a later court. The provision, as you envision it, will be located within a larger contract that sets up the employment relationship with the junior dentist.

> This probationary period is intended to allow [junior dentist] to develop the confidence and trust of the patients of Chris Colgate, DDS in anticipation of the transfer of Colgate's practice to [junior dentist]. The trust exposes Chris Colgate to the danger that, if things don't work out, [junior dentist] will leave and, having built trust with Colgate's patients, destroy Colgate's patient base.

> Accordingly, in consideration of Colgate's agreement to employ junior dentist and encourage him/her to develop trust with Colgate's patients, [junior dentist] agrees that, for a period of one year following departure from Colgate's practice, [junior dentist] will not treat any of Colgate's patients that 1) exist at the time of [junior dentist's] departure and 2) reside within a radius of 3 miles from Colgate's office location.

The foregoing reflects your view about the kind of provision that will protect Chris against unfair competition from a junior dentist. It is conservative, but your view is that Chris is better off with a provision that is likely to be enforced rather than one that "pushes the envelope." The junior dentist *might* be given special protection from no compete provisions, given the interests of their patients. And in our jurisdiction, an overbroad no-compete agreement is simply void, so we don't want to take chances. Moreover, given the focus on the hardship to the younger dentist, you cannot even guarantee that a very conservative provision will be enforced — that will depend on future facts about the junior's hardship that we cannot know at this point.

Chris has returned and you have presented your solution to Chris. Chris has what she thinks is a better idea. She thinks she can get a young dentist to sign just about anything because it is very hard to start off in

---

[5] Comment 2 explains "Paragraph (b) prohibits a lawyer from agreeing not to represent other persons in connection with settling a claim on behalf of a client."

dental practice on one's own and, since people have been putting off dental work during the local recession, dental jobs are scarce. Chris is now far more focused on her desire that she not waste time on a junior dentist who works for her for awhile and then simply leaves voluntarily. She is, at this point, far less worried about the junior dentist stealing patients.

Chris's primary goal now is to keep the junior dentist on the job, even if he or she wants to quit. She has asked you to revise the provision so it prevents the junior dentist from working at dentistry anywhere in the State for a period of 10 years after leaving Chris's employ. This conversation has ensued:

> YOU: Chris, this is going to be a real problem. As you directed, I've not done a great deal of research on this. But I can tell you with nearly 100% certainty that what you're talking about will clearly violate the public policy of this State and not be enforceable at all.

> CHRIS: Enforcement, schmenforcement. I just want the person to stay on the job and if they *think* they can't work anywhere else if they quit, they'll stay. I know I run the risk of no enforcement if the person leaves but, with this provision, they're not going to leave and I'm willing to take the chance.

> YOU: You want to comply with the law, don't you?

> CHRIS: We both know that this provision is clearly unenforceable: so what? The law doesn't matter: if the dentist *thinks* he has to stay on the job, the provision does its work. And if you draft it to look "legal," the dentist will think it's enforceable.

Professional Responsibility Limits on Drafting:

Many people think of the lawyer as a simple extension of the client, a professional whose job is to implement whatever the client wants. But this has never been the case. Outside of the realm of lawyer discipline, civil and criminal sanctions can attach to the work of a transactional lawyer and "the client made me do it" is never a defense. For example, a lawyer who follows a client's orders and drafts a contract to extort money can be criminally liable along with the client for extortion. The lawyer who creates the documents through which the client commits fraud can be liable criminally in some cases, and can be held liable with the client in civil actions by the victims. Assisting a client in violating the rules governing bankruptcy can expose the lawyer to criminal liability for a "bankruptcy crime." This is, by no means, an exclusive list.

These same kinds of activities that expose a lawyer to criminal and civil liability can also expose a lawyer to professional discipline. Rule 1.2(d) provides:

(d) A lawyer shall not counsel a client to engage, or assist a client, in conduct that the lawyer knows is criminal or fraudulent . . . .

Task Two:

Given what you've just learned about the limits of your own representation in this context, do you think you *could* draft the provision Chris has suggested? Rule 1.2(d) is expressed in terms of your knowledge. Do you *know* that Chris's conduct is "*criminal or fraudulent*"?

One way to think about ethical limitations is to imagine a smart, aggressive disciplinary counsel who doesn't like you, is out to ruin you, and knows everything that you know. Please write down the essential facts behind an ethics complaint against you for drafting the provision sought by Chris. After you have written your answer, consult Self-Assessment 2 for Exercise H on the LexisNexis web course.

Once a lawyer has discovered that she cannot do what the client wants her to do, the real difficulties begin: how does one handle a client in this situation? The polar choices are 1) to do what the client wants anyway and hope to avoid sanctions (most good lawyers would say this is a bad idea) or 2) withdrawing from representation (many good lawyers would also say this is a bad idea, at least until other possibilities are tried). Depending on the situation, there may be many choices for the lawyer between these outer limits. The choices that lawyers make in these situations will, over time, define the kind of lawyers that they become.

Task Three:

Think about the choices in between 1) risking it by simply doing what the client asks, and 2) losing the client through withdrawal from representation. Also think about what you would need to know in order to take the best approach to dealing with Chris. Write down 1) what you might like to know and 2) three or four approaches you might take to the situation. After you have written your answer, consult Self-Assessment 3 for Exercise H on the LexisNexis web course.

Task Four:

Let's extend this examination of drafting ethics by looking at an all-to-common problem.

Imagine you represent a furniture seller in a low income part of town. That seller provides financing to its buyers by taking "security interests" in the things that it sells to its buyers. You have been asked to review and update the client's form contracts for making these sales.

One of the provisions within the client's current form contract is a "cross-collateralization clause." Through this clause, the buyer purports to give to the seller a security interest in everything the buyer has ever bought from the seller, whether those things have been "paid off" or not. All those earlier purchases will thus stand as collateral for the current purchase. The effect of this provision, *if it were enforceable*, is to give the seller the right to "replevy" (that is, to repossess) every item the buyer ever bought from the seller for a single missed payment on the current purchase. This, in turn, creates great leverage for the seller to induce payment.

But the provision is *not* enforceable in many contracts. Since the 1970's federal and state law has made such provisions unenforceable in consumer contracts.[6]

Consider the following material in preparation for your analysis:

In a very provocative article, *The Ethics of Invalid and "Iffy" Contract Clauses,* 40 LOY. L.A. L. REV. 487 (2006), Professor Christina Kuntz examines the kinds of questions we have here. She quotes material from another source that is germane to our inquiry:

> The highest court of State recently held that a certain clause in a consumer goods contract is unconscionable and therefore unenforceable. A retail store in State nevertheless insists that its lawyer, L, continue to include the clause in its contracts, on the grounds that the great majority of consumers will not know it is unenforceable and thus will comply with its terms anyway. . . .
>
> The Proposed Final Draft of Rule 1.2(d) . . . included language that would have prohibited the preparation of an instrument 'containing terms the lawyer knows or reasonably should know are legally prohibited.' The ABA House of Delegates deleted this provision, however, before promulgation of the Model Rules in 1983. The Ethics 2000 Commission . . . did not recommend restoration of the deleted text. Given this drafting history, it would seem that L could not now be disciplined merely for including the unconscionable clause in the contract.
>
> On the other hand, if the clause is likely to mislead customers as to their rights, use of the clause might be held to constitute fraud. If so, the general prohibition in Rule 1.2(d) against assisting in fraud would again be applicable.
>
> L might seek to dissuade his client from including the clause, bringing to bear moral and other nonlegal concerns, as contemplated by Rule 2.1 .... L might point out, for example, that continued inclusion of the unconscionable clause could result in

---

[6] An early case that you may read in the Contracts course is *Williams v. Walker-Thomas Furniture Co.*, 350 F.2d 445 (D.C. Cir. 1965) (cross-collateralization provision in a furniture-financing contract may be held unconscionable under District of Columbia law).

class action liability and adverse publicity if the practice is challenged in court or criticized in the media. L might also resign or threaten to resign, pointing to his right under Rule 1.16(b)(4) to withdraw if the client 'insists upon pursuing an objective that the lawyer considers repugnant or with which the lawyer has a fundamental disagreement ....' Most clients would treat seriously the views of a trusted counselor who was willing to resign over a matter of principle.

Christina Kuntz., *The Ethics of Invalid and "Iffy" Contract Clauses*, 40 Loy. L.A. L. Rev. 487, 496-97 (2006), *quoting* Jeffrey C. Hazard and W. William Hodes, The Law of Lawyering, §5.12, illus. 5-13 (3d ed. 2001-2005).

Assuming that you see the cross-collateralization clause in your review of the form contract and that you know it is unambiguously unenforceable, can you leave it in? How is our situation different from that in the hypothetical posed by Professors Hazard and Hodes? Write out a short answer. After you have written your answer, consult Self-Assessment 4 for Exercise H on the LexisNexis web course.

Chapter 9
CONTROLLING RISK IN PURCHASES AND ACQUISITIONS I: REAL ESTATE PURCHASE

PREVIEW

We have designed this Chapter to teach something about using contracts to control risk. There is almost no limit on the creativity of lawyers in their use of contracts (not all to the good, as some of the more exotic financial contracts at the center of recent economic problems have demonstrated) but to develop that creativity, you have to be faced with a problem that demands a little of it. We have chosen a residential real estate transaction as the vehicle for this exercise. This allows us to give you a look at how contracts, and the lawyers who use them, function in this corner of commercial life.

The Chapter progresses in a building-block fashion. It begins with a *very* simple first task designed to foster understanding of the many ways persons might control the riskiness of their purchases and concludes with an exercise in drafting a modern inspection contingency clause.

SUBSTANTIVE CONTENT:

- Options as risk controllers
- Conditions as risk-controllers
- Overview of residential real estate practice

SKILLS AND VALUES UTILIZED:

- Methods business people and lawyers use to control risk in asset purchases
- Use of fact representations and warranties as to future performance to adjust risk
- Analyzing different contract provisions that are closely related
- Drafting options and conditions

ESTIMATED TIME FOR COMPLETION: 60 Minutes

LEVEL OF DIFFICULTY (1 to 5):

A Brief Introduction to Residential Real Estate Acquisitions:

Real estate practice varies widely among U.S. jurisdictions. A real estate sale is the seller's exchange (or conveyance) of title to real estate to the buyer for a price; the real estate contract is the agreement by which the buyer and seller agree to the terms of that exchange and agree to make it. We will describe here the basic framework. You should recognize that what you see in your state could vary in the details from what is described here.

The simple sounding transaction described above is actually quite complicated owing in part to the "extra" participants. Few people have the cash to buy a house and many sellers do not own their houses outright. Buyers usually need to borrow money from a lender who will take a mortgage on the purchased property and sellers will often owe money on the mortgage created when they bought the house they are now selling. This means that the seller's mortgage holder wants to get paid while its borrower still has the house, and that some of the money to pay the seller's lender will come from the buyer's lender. The buyer will be interested in extinguishing the seller's bank's mortgage on the property, and the buyer's bank will want to place its mortgage on the property before the buyer gets it.[1] Companies, called title insurance companies, insure the old and new owner's title, protecting against hidden interests that might adversely affect the title. They also often function as escrow agents, holding the buyer's down payment and distributing the purchase money to those entitled to it.

The real estate sales contract forms when the seller accepts the buyer's offer to purchase or the buyer accepts the seller's offer to sell. There then passes a period of time prior to the closing or, sometimes called settlement. This meeting of the parties is when an acquisition agreement, like a real estate sale, is actually performed — when the money and deed to the property actually change hands. Some of the money at the "settlement table" will come from the buyer's bank and some from the buyer; some of the money will go to the seller's bank and some to the seller. The deed will go from seller to buyer and the

---

[1] The "mortgage" is an interest in the real estate conveyed by the *mortgagor*, i.e., the owner (who is usually the borrower), to the *mortgagee*, i.e., the lender. The mortgage stands as security for the borrower's obligation: if the borrower defaults, the law permits the mortgagee to *foreclose* the mortgage. The traditional approach calls for the mortgagee to sell the owner's property at a *sheriff's* or *foreclosure* sale, pay itself out of the proceeds and return any remainder to the borrower. Many states have now streamlined foreclosure by dispensing with the judicial procedure. This is a complicated subject that you can examine in courses in *Secured Transactions* or *Real Estate Finance*.

title insurance company will typically deliver its title policy to the buyer at the closing.[2]

All this complexity requires an expert or experts in the process to make it move efficiently. In some states, the involvement of a lawyer in a residential real estate sale is routine;[3] others use real estate brokers to bring the technical expertise into the exchange process. Individuals will sometimes hire lawyers to represent them in residential real estate deals if the property is big enough or if they have any reason to be anxious about the transaction.

In real life, the transaction that follows would likely be governed by a contract form prepared by the local real estate industry and that written contract would likely govern many of the problems raised here. We have vastly over-simplified the exercise because the point is not to teach real estate transactions but to look at controlling risk through contract terms within such transactions. To understand the more important last parts of the exercise, you must complete the first parts, even if they seem overly-simple and artificial — it's a step-by-step progression. In another Chapter you can look at one of the common roles of a lawyer in a more-complicated (but still simple) business acquisition.

EXERCISE I:

Marty, an *extremely naïve and gullible* consumer buyer, has entered the real estate market and has finally found a house, new on the market, that she likes that is being sold by the owner. She's buying the house from a distance and cannot look at it but likes the photos. She wants to reduce the riskiness of buying the house. In her naivete, she decides to approach the seller via e-mail. She asks specifically, "does this house have termites." The seller replies "no" which is what the seller believes to be true. On the strength of that statement, Marty buys the house.

Task One: Factual Representations that turn out to be false

Marty has come to you for legal advice. A month after the closing, she finally viewed her purchase and began preparing the house for move-in. Soon after her arrival, she learned the house was, in fact, infested with termites. It would require a considerable expense to repair the damage and exterminate the termites. Instead of going through all that trouble, Marty wants to get her money back, and return the house to the seller. Before you decide what to recommend, (call the

---

[2] All acquisition transactions follow the same pattern: the contract forms, time passes, and contract is performed at the closing. The acquisition of a business, while structurally the same, is immensely more complicated. It can take the participants a long time just to execute all the documents!

[3] New Jersey is such a state. *See, e.g., Sears Mortgage Co. v. Michael Rose and Emily Kaiser*, 134 N.J. 326, 1993 N.J. LEXIS 739 (1993).

seller to negotiate, litigate, lump it, etc.,)[4] you need to assess what Marty's rights are and, in particular, whether she can reverse the sale.[5] Please go to Lexis.com on the Web and, using Get a Document, bring up *LaCourse v. Kiesel*, 77 A. 2d 877 (Pa. 1951). Skim through that case and then write your opinion in a couple of sentences. After you have written your answer, consult Self-Assessment 1 for Exercise I on the LexisNexis web course.

Performance Warranties

No doubt you have passed "for sale" signs in front of houses that have the word "warranty" written on them. What the seller is advertising is a commitment (usually from a third party) to repair or replace components of the house that fail during the warranty period. Performance warranties are most common with automobiles — "if it fails within 50,000 miles, we'll fix it" — but you also find them in real estate sales, particularly in new construction.

When sold with a house, these warranties[6] are contractual commitments by the warrantor to do whatever the warranty provides. Since the warranty *is* simply a contract, that contract defines what the warranty product is, that is, what it covers, against what problems, and for how long. When developing this kind of product, there is a tremendous economic temptation to hide limitations and qualifications within the small print. So it is essential to know clearly what the warranty provides and what its limits are. And since ordinary promises (for example "performance warranties") can be extinguished through bankruptcy, it is important to have some confidence that the warrantor will be financially able to perform during the warranty period.

Let's suppose that, instead of the "no termites" representation, Marty decided to reduce her purchase risk by getting the seller to provide, in writing: "I promise that I will repair the house should it require repairs for which buyer receives an estimate in excess of $100, for a period of two years from the date of the sale."

---

[4] You will learn that the fact the buyer has rights does not mean that she has the means to exercise them through a court of law. But even if a client is not financially able to litigate, learning her rights is important because they serve as a foundation for designing a strategy to effectively deal with the client's problem. Litigation is *seldom* the solution to a legal problem but how litigation will probably turn out often factors into the non-litigation solution.

[5] For purposes here, assume that rescission of the completed sale is an available remedy. A complicated thicket of contract, property, and civil procedure law sometimes bars rescission of an acquisition once it has "closed." We leave the details to upper-class courses in real estate transactions and mergers and acquisitions.

[6] The law sometimes affixes "implied warranties" to various kinds of sales, the most common being the implied warranties in sales of goods transactions covered by the Uniform Commercial Code, UCC §§ 2-313, 2-314, and 2-315. The performance warranty described in the text would be an "express warranty" and would be approached like most other contracts unless, of course, the jurisdiction had chosen to regulate them. This is a distinct possibility because, for obvious reasons, they resemble insurance, a "product" that is very highly regulated.

It's clear that Marty has reduced risk here by obtaining a repair warranty but, once again, this may not be the best protection she can get for protecting herself against a bad purchase. Should the seller not voluntarily perform, the buyer will have to use the law to force compliance or obtain damages. In the case of, at least relatively, minor repairs (< $10,000), the costs of litigation could easily exceed the costs of repair thereby making the warranty relatively worthless.

It should be obvious by now that the best way for the buyer to reduce the riskiness of this purchase is to make a detailed assessment of the property *before* actually closing the contract. This would involve ensuring beforehand, for example, that there are no termites, that the heating system works well, that the plumbing is in good shape, that the roof does not require repair, and so on. Depending on the house and the prospective buyer, this kind of risk reduction can require some level of expertise in order to do it right. While some contemporary buyers are competent to assess the quality of real property themselves, for at least the past 20 years, the practice has been for buyers to hire experts to make this assessment for them. For a distant buyer like Marty, this would probably be a necessity.

Experts cost money, sometimes a lot of money. Marty could have hired an expert to make her assessment prior to *making* the contract, but doing so would have exposed Marty to the risk of losing the property after she has expended money on assessing the quality of the purchase. It would be better to have the seller committed to the sale so that if the inspection confirmed a good investment, the buyer could follow through with it.

One way a buyer could accomplish this is to get an option to buy the property from the seller. The Restatement of Contracts (Second) § 25 supplies a good definition of an option contract:

> An option contract is a promise which meets the requirements for the formation of a contract and limits the promisor's power to revoke an offer.

While the matter is complicated, the seller's promise not to revoke an offer to sell - the essence of an option contract in this context - generally requires consideration in order to be binding. In a case like this, the buyer would have to pay for the option.

Task Two: Draft an option on the property

Let us suppose the seller is willing to sell the house for $200,000. Marty may well be willing to buy it for that price provided her expert's examination shows that there are no big problems. It will take her a week to have the examination done and to digest the report. Marty wants to offer to pay the seller $100 for seller to make a one-week irrevocable offer to sell for $200,000. As Marty's lawyer, you would draft the seller's irrevocable offer and present it to the seller.[7] Draft a simple option provision with which to propose such a deal to the seller and then compare that proposed option language with the example provided in the self-assessment. After you have written your answer, consult Self-Assessment 2 for Exercise I on the LexisNexis web course.

Task Three: Implications of the option approach

Recall that seller has just placed this house on the market. Why, given that fact, might the seller be reluctant to agree to the option solution to the buyer's inspection problem? After you have written your answer, consult Self-Assessment 3 for Exercise I on the LexisNexis web course.

The shortcomings of the option approach take us to a final approach, the one that is now dominant in real estate sales practice in many parts of the country. The parties might make their contract for sale but, almost always at the buyer's insistence, condition the closing of the sale in some way on the results of an inspection by an expert that will take place within some time limit. This, of course, exposes the seller to the risk that the sale will unravel via a "bad" inspection report, but sellers seem to prefer the security of having *some* commitment by the buyer over the option situation where they are committed but the buyer is not.

This kind of condition, or "contingency" as it is often known in the trade, has great flexibility in apportioning risk. At one extreme, an inspection contingency clause could require that the inspection be "satisfactory to buyer" and thereby place a great deal of risk on the seller. This is because virtually any defect, and there are inevitably defects in both new and old homes, gives the buyer a way out of the contract.[8] At the opposite extreme, the contingency could be drafted so that it would be triggered only if the expert certifies that repairs will cost in excess of $X. If drafted correctly, this will mean that, for any repair that will cost less than X to make, the buyer will have to absorb the cost of making that repair.

---

[7] It can be confusing but suffice it to say that the person or entity that makes an offer, an acceptance, an option, or other contractual move need not be the person who drafts it. In our case, Marty is driving the negotiation and knows what she needs from the seller. It would make little sense under those circumstances for her *not* to draft the seller's irrevocable offer. Moreover, by controlling the initial language of a writing, the drafter seizes a negotiating advantage that is nearly always worth the effort, or legal fees, that go into it.

[8] As you may learn in your course work, courts can interpret "personal satisfaction" clauses either using a subjective standard (good faith — that is "honest dissatisfaction") or an objective standard ("reasonable dissatisfaction"). Which standard a court will use will depend on how the provision is expressed and the context. While a reasonableness standard will place greater constraints on the buyer, suffice it to say that either standard will give the buyer a great deal of power to avoid the sale.

Task Four: Think through the elements of an inspection contingency clause

Giving the buyer the right to have the property inspected before the closing is a good solution to the risks of a purchase but such a provision is far more complicated than might first appear. Think about it: seller will be taking his home off the market and does not want the sale to fail. In addition, seller knows that *anyone* can find flaws in a piece of real estate and doesn't want the sale to fail for trifling "defects." Finally, seller wants this process to be over quickly so that, if this sale fails, he can get the house back on the market quickly. As with any drafting, one needs to think through the substance before the drafting begins. Please make a list of the issues or problems that you think should be addressed in an inspection contingency clause. After you have made your list, consult Self-Assessment 4 for Exercise I on the LexisNexis web course. The Self-Assessment will give you some examples of these provisions from residential real estate contracts.

Task Five: Real life experience with inspection contingency clauses

Either

Read *Outsmarting the Negotiation Process* (on the LexisNexis web course) and follow the other directions that are appended to that short essay.

OR

Listen to the Podcast interview of a Philadelphia real estate agent (on the LexisNexis web course) who talks about her experiences with inspection contingency clauses in that particular market.

The Self-Assessment 5 for Exercise I is located on the LexisNexis web course.

Chapter 10

CONTROLLING RISK IN PURCHASES AND ACQUISITIONS II: LAWYER DUE DILIGENCE

PREVIEW

In Chapter 9, we considered a few ways one could use contract provisions to control risk in a simple setting where a person is acquiring residential real estate. One could ask the seller to make "representations" about different aspects of the property (e.g., this property is termite free"). The typical consequence of a materially false representation is the buyer's ability to unravel the sale. The buyer also could have the seller promise to repair defective appliances or parts of the property (e.g., "should an appliance fail within one year, we will repair it at no cost to you"), that is, to make a "warranty."[1] Finally, the buyer could find out for herself what she needs to know by examining the property, usually through the services of an expert, before closing the purchase - that is, before exchanging money for the deed.

While the residential real property examination normally does not require legal expertise, creating the time to make such an examination while holding the pending sale together may require a lawyer. In Chapter 9 we considered, alternatively, the use of an option on the property and the addition of an inspection contingency clause to the contract of sale to control risks for the buyer. Because the latter was preferable for a variety of reasons, our final focus was on creating a provision that posed acceptable risk both to the seller and to the buyer.

Although the game gets bigger and vastly more complicated when someone is buying a business rather than a house, the underlying dynamics are the same. Lawyers use "reps and warranties" to apportion the risks that are inevitable in such a purchase and they participate far more directly in the "inspection" that the buyer conducts before purchasing the business.

As with the real estate contract, the buyer's lawyers can use various devices to create the time for the buyer to evaluate what is being purchased. As in the simpler residential real estate context, the buyer

---

[1] The distinction between "representations" and "warranties" is not nearly so clear in practice. If a seller says "this thing will work for 10 years," is that a representation of fact or a commitment as to future performance? Lawyers fudge the problem by including "representations and warranties" in one breath or part of their contracts without thinking much about them. Thinking about them as performing different functions and delivering different relief to buyers is useful in fine-tuning risk. In purchases of assets other than goods, sellers rarely make warranties.

could (but seldom *would*) purchase an option to buy the business,[2] or could execute a sales contract but condition the closing on a set of contingencies that the buyer would define. In this more sophisticated context, lawyers may use a "letter of intent," to create some minimal level of party commitment to the deal while the parties evaluate what is being conveyed.[3] A letter of intent is, generally speaking, a vague commitment to go forward that may or not be a contract, depending on the intent of the parties and whether consideration has been exchanged. You may encounter a "letter of intent" case in your classroom work and would certainly encounter them in real world practice.

Our focus in this exercise is not on the contract methods used to create the evaluation period. Rather, it is on the lawyer's participation in the inspection that follows, an activity that also requires knowledge of contract law. In this exercise, you will actually perform "due diligence" on a small part of a business acquisition. The context will be a simple one but the point is to give you a sense of the work and how pervasive it is.

SUBSTANTIVE CONTENT:

- Introduction to Lawyer due diligence
- Introduction to the intangible assets and liabilities that usually accompany a business acquisition.

SKILLS AND VALUES UTILIZED:

- Performing simple due diligence on selected parts of a commercial real estate lease
- Reading and interpreting provisions of a commercial real estate lease

---

[2] Comment from Philadelphia Lawyer Matthew Cole Esq.:

> [I]t is extremely rare for a buyer of a business (asset purchase transaction) to purchase an option, though a letter of intent may contain what amounts to an option: the "no-shop" clause. This prevents the seller from soliciting other purchasers or even entertaining inquiries from unsolicited purchasers for a period of time (60–90 days is customary). In basic asset purchase transactions, it would be unusual, however, to pay for the no shop clause. In such transactions, even obtaining a "no shop" clause may be very difficult for a buyer.

[3] **Sidebar on Local Asset Purchase Practice**
Matthew Cole, Esq., describes the smaller asset purchase procedure in the Philadelphia PA region as follows (the practice could be different in other localities):
The standard procedure for smaller asset purchase transactions is:
1. Enter into a mostly non-binding letter of intent (except for confidentiality regarding the seller's data, the no shop clause - if used - and a few other items) or term sheet signed by both seller and purchaser followed by an asset purchase agreement. Due diligence is often conducted during the letter of intent term period, as the asset purchase agreement is being negotiated; or
2. Commence due diligence without a letter of intent and negotiate the asset purchase agreement simultaneously.
While real estate sales usually involve signing a purchase agreement followed by an inspection period for the buyer, asset purchase transactions do not necessarily follow this model. In fact, when representing buyers, I have often structured the transaction to avoid that scenario. I like to have the agreement signed and close simultaneously. The due diligence is conducted while the asset purchase agreement is being negotiated. I would much rather walk from a deal before an agreement is signed than run the risk that the seller will claim that the deal was in fact finalized despite the inspection period "out" in the agreement and that the buyer, my client, breached.

ESTIMATED TIME FOR COMPLETION: 45 Minutes

LEVEL OF DIFFICULTY (1 to 5):

EXERCISE J:

Your client is an individual who is interested in buying a local hardware store business. The business assets consist of a long-term lease on the physical premises, the inventory (against which the current owner may have borrowed some money), the store fixtures, and the hardware store's name and reputation which are quite good. While the store has had long-term relationships with its inventory suppliers, these relationships are not contractual. The business also has two loyal employees who have each worked there for over 10 years. The owner has set a price of $250,000[4] to purchase the business. Your client has a romantic image of himself running a hardware store and this old-fashioned store fits the image perfectly. The client can get the purchase price together but, of course, needs to know what he's getting before he can assess whether this is a deal worth doing.

The business side of this deal involves, among other things, 1) assessing the value of the assets and determining whether the price is appropriate for the assets (the same assessment that one performs when one purchases anything), and 2) assessing whether what is being purchased is adequate to generate an acceptable return on the price as an investment.

Not included in this exercise is the legal drafting part of the exchange which involves 1) using a contract device to create a time period within which to evaluate the assets without exposing the client to excessive risk, and 2) drafting an agreement that apportions the risks in the way the parties wish.

Lawyer Due Diligence:

Unlike the real estate inspection that would be conducted by a real estate expert or engineer, the "inspection" in a business acquisition is almost always orchestrated and mostly conducted by lawyers. This kind of

---

[4] According to Matthew Cole, Esq., "I would say $250,000 is about as small as would be economical, even for a solo practitioner to handle who has the appropriate skills for the task."

legal work, which accompanies nearly every business acquisition of any size, has come to be known in the trade as performing due diligence. Due diligence is a very common task for business lawyers, particularly those in the early years of their careers; in larger deals, performing due diligence absorbs teams of many lawyers and requires considerable organizational and management skills in addition to legal skills.

As you might expect, in more complicated acquisition agreements, the lawyer's due diligence usually involves spotting the legal issues implicated in the various assets being transferred, and then knowing what is needed in order to resolve those issues. Some issues can be resolved by more factual investigation, some through legal research. Others might be satisfactorily resolved by adding representations or warranties into the agreement, and still others might be resolved by negotiations.

For an illustration in a simple context, let us return to the hardware store problem. If the store's inventory were being sold along with the hardware store, the buyer, of course, would want to understand how much that inventory represented of the overall price of the business, and whether that was a good or a bad price. But to make that assessment, the owner would have to know whether the seller held the inventory free and clear of the claims of others or, alternatively, whether it might be encumbered, that is, subject to others' prior claims. The seller could represent that it was not, or agree to indemnify the buyer if it was, but such statements of fact or commitments might not be good enough for the buyer.[5]

A lawyer could contribute to the risk assessment by examining, for example, whether others might have prior claims to the inventory.[6] This would be the case if lenders held valid security interests, or if others had simply consigned parts of the inventory to the store owner for resale. If it turned out that the inventory was subject to earlier claims, the value the buyer was acquiring would be lower than he might have thought. If exposure to prior claims were found, the due diligence to-do list that might emerge from this part of the investigation could include "lower the offering price," "get the seller to pay off the lender," "negotiate with the lender," "get the seller to guarantee the debt secured by the inventory," etc., etc.

As another example, the client would want to learn whether the store had outstanding liability claims against it. A representation by the seller in the contract that there were no known claims would help,

---

[5]   If, after the sale, the buyer encountered problems that the seller would not voluntarily fix, it could cost the buyer a good deal in legal fees to force compliance or obtain a damage equivalent. The purchaser of residential real estate wants to know what she is getting *before* advancing the money. Many purchasers of businesses want the same thing to the extent they can get it. That is why they perform due diligence instead of depending on the word (or even contractual commitments) of the seller.

[6]   A lawyer can often do this by consulting some public record. Like the real estate inspector who knows about plumbing, the business lawyer adds her expertise to the mix by knowing which public records to consult and what to look for in them. In this case, a search would likely be done in the Uniform Commercial Code (UCC) filing office, typically in the State capital. An appropriate search would reveal whether the seller of the business used the inventory as collateral for a loan and, if so, who held the "security interest" in the inventory.

but the due diligence work would likely also involve a search of the records (lawyers hire services to do this), or an online search if one were available. If the due diligence work uncovered claims, the buyer's lawyer might consider whether those claims would be valid against the new client-owner and, if so, the viability of those claims and their value. The lawyer might also, or instead, consider how to control that issue within the acquisition agreement. Clearly, no business buyer wants to buy a lawsuit[7] along with the business; in a transaction of the size in this problem, most buyers would walk from the sale rather than take even a small risk that the litigation was viable. But the more general point – and the point of lawyer due diligence – is to know with some level of accuracy exactly what the client is buying.

A lawyer would offer professional views about the tax aspects of the acquisition or, if the store were a corporation, about the corporate issues (e.g., who in the seller's corporation has the power to sign the sales agreement) that might be implicated by the sale.

It is easy to imagine how complicated the lawyer's due diligence task might be even in our simple hardware store acquisition example. Our object here is simply to acquaint you with this kind of lawyer task and give you a sense of what is involved.

Task One:

Let us assume some additional facts.

The seller's hardware store has been prosperous partly because it is located on a highly-visible and accessible corner of the town. This location, our client believes, is central to the store's future potential; without it, the client will probably not want to move forward. But the hardware store seller does not own the real estate; it rents it, through a long-term lease.

In the negotiations the seller has told the client buyer that the land-lord will let the store stay on that corner "forever" and has committed never to raise the rent by more than 3% per year. You have told the buyer-client to get a copy of the commercial lease for the store or you have requested one directly from the seller. That lease is printed below. **Please focus your due diligence only on Paragraphs 3, 12, and the signature pages.**[8] Lawyers who perform due diligence must understand every word of the document they are working on so be sure

---

[7] We use the colloquial expression "buy a lawsuit" here to mean acquiring a *liability* along with the business. This is the way the expression is normally used. Nonetheless, technically, one could buy either side of a lawsuit. Thus, the buyer could acquire a *claim* against others in the course of buying a business. The simplest form of this would be the business's accounts receivable, that is, debts to the business of others who have not yet paid. There is lawyer work here too — if the claims against others are being counted as "assets" by the seller in the acquisition, are they properly valued? How viable are the claims? What do they represent in dollars? Might *they* be encumbered? What are the chances of collecting on them?

[8] In a real case, buyer's lawyer would comb through the whole lease and make a list of all the legal issues she thought might be implicated, and then begin to resolve those issues through more information or through negotiations.

to look up any words in these provisions that you do not understand. You should also read through the rest of the lease so you will get a taste of what a commercial lease might contain and the due diligence that would be implicated in reviewing the entire lease.

Once you think you understand the language of the provisions in question, make 1) a list of the legal problems that you think are triggered by those three parts of the lease and 2) a to-do list of what needs to be done in order to resolve those problems. Once you have done that, consult Self-Assessment 1 for Exercise J on the LexisNexis Web Course.

LEASE[9]

LEASE (this "Lease"), dated December _, [ThisYear – 1], is made by and between **Sam Seller** (together with its successors-in-interest, "Lessor") and Learned Landlord, Inc, a New York corporation ("Lessee").

NOW, THEREFORE, in consideration of the mutual promises contained in this Lease, the parties, intending to be legally bound by this Lease, agree as follows:

1. Premises. Lessor leases to Lessee and Lessee leases from Lessor for the Initial Term (as defined below), at the rental, and upon all of the conditions set forth herein, that certain real property consisting of a one-story space of approximately 90 feet by 200 feet in the building known as Sam's Hardware, in Fulton County, State of New York (together with all land and all improvements thereon, the "Premises"), as described fully on Exhibit A attached hereto.

2. Term.

2.1. Initial Term. The initial term of this Lease shall commence on January 1, [ThisYear] (the "Lease Commencement Date") and shall expire on December 31, [ThisYear+3] (the "Expiration Date") (unless sooner terminated pursuant to any Lease provision, the "Term").

2.2. Delay in Possession. If for any reason Lessor cannot deliver possession of the Premises to Lessee on the Lease Commencement Date, Lessor shall not be subject to any liability therefore, nor shall such failure affect the validity of this Lease or the obligations of Lessee hereunder or extend the Term, but in such case, the Lease Commencement Date shall be postponed to the date upon which Lessor does tender possession.

3. Rent; Other Lessee Monetary Obligations.

3.1 Base Rent. During the term of this Lease, Lessee shall pay to Lessor, at the office of Lessor, or at such other place or places designated by Lessor from time to time, without any prior demand, and without any deduction or offset, as monthly rent, the following amounts ("Base Rent") for the time periods listed:

---

[9] This lease was prepared by Matthew Cole, Esq. and is used with his permission.

LEASE YEAR	MONTHLY BASE RENT
First Lease Year (January 1, [ThisYear] to December 31, [ThisYear])	Three Thousand One Hundred Dollars ($3,100)
Second Lease Year (January 1, [ThisYear+1] to December 31, [ThisYear+1])	Three Thousand One Hundred Dollars ($3,100)
Third Lease Year (January 1, [ThisYear+2] to December 31, [ThisYear+2])	Three Thousand Two Hundred Dollars ($3,200)
Fourth Lease Year (January 1, [ThisYear+3] to December 31, [ThisYear+3])	Three Thousand Two Hundred Dollars ($3,200)

Base Rent is payable on the first day of each calendar month during the term of this Lease, commencing on the Lease Commencement Date. Rent shall be payable in lawful money of the United States.

4. Condition of Premises "AS IS". Lessee accepts the Premises in its current condition "AS IS," subject to all applicable zoning, municipal, county, state and federal laws, ordinances, statutes, rules and regulations governing and regulating the use and occupancy of the Premises, and any covenants or restrictions, and accepts this Lease subject thereto. Lessee acknowledges that Lessor and Lesson's agents and employees have not made any representation or warranty as to the present or future suitability of the Premises for the conduct of Lessee's business.

5. Security Deposit. Lessee will deposit with Lessor upon execution of this Lease Nine Thousand Three Hundred Dollars ($9,300) hereto as security for Lessee's faithful performance of Lessee's obligations hereunder (the "Security Deposit"). If Lessee fails to pay Base Rent, Additional Rent (as defined below) or other charges due under this Lease, or otherwise defaults with respect to any provision of this Lease, Lessor may use, apply or retain all or any portion of the Security Deposit for the payment of any rent or other charge in default or for the payment of any other sum to which Lessor may become obligated by reason of Lessee's default, or to compensate Lessor for any loss or damage which Lessor may suffer thereby. Lessor shall not be required to keep the Security Deposit separate from its general accounts. If Lessee performs all of Lessee's obligations hereunder, the Security Deposit, or so much thereof as has not theretofore been applied by Lessor, shall be returned, without payment of interest or other increment for its use, to Lessee (or, at Lessor's option, to the last permitted assignee, if any, of Lessee's interest hereunder) at the expiration of the term hereof, and after Lessee has vacated the Premises. No trust relationship is created herein between Lessor and Lessee with respect to said Security Deposit. In no event shall Lessee use or attempt to use the Security Deposit for the payment of Base Rent or Additional Rent during the Lease term or for the payment of any of the foregoing with respect to the last month of the Lease term.

6. Use. The Premises shall be used and occupied solely for the purpose of selling tools and other goods customarily sold in a hardware store. If Lessee's activities at the Premises result in any increase in the cost of insurance for the Premises to Lessor, including, by way of example and not of limitation, any increase in fire insurance premiums, Lessee shall bear the cost of all such increases and shall pay Lessor such amounts promptly upon demand by Lessor. During the Term, Lessee will comply with all laws, rules or regulations of any governmental authority to which it is subject.

7. Maintenance, Repairs and Alterations. Lessee shall keep in good order, condition and repair the Premises and every part thereof, structural and non-structural, (whether or not such portion of the Premises requiring repair, or the means of repairing the same are reasonably or readily accessible to Lessee, and whether or not the need for such repairs occurs as a result of Lessee's use, any prior use, acts of God, the natural elements or the age of such portion of the Premises) including, by way of example and not of limitation, all plumbing, heating, air conditioning within the Premises, fixtures, interior and exterior walls (including painting), foundations, ceilings, roofs (interior and exterior), subroofs, floors, subfloors, windows, doors, plate glass and skylights located within the Premises, and all landscaping, driveways, parking lots, fences and signs located on the Premises and sidewalks and parkways adjacent to the Premises. Lessee shall defend, hold harmless and indemnify Lessor against costs or losses (including Lessor's legal fees) arising from any mechanics' or materialmens' lien against the Premises resulting from any alteration of the Premises by Lessee. Lessee shall defend, hold harmless and indemnify Lessor against costs or losses (including Lessor's legal fees) arising from any mechanics' or materialmens' lien against the Premises resulting from any alteration of the Premises by Lessee. If Lessee fails to perform Lessee's obligations under this Section 7, or under any other section of this Lease, Lessor may at its sole option (but shall not be required to) enter upon the Premises during business hours (or, in the case of an emergency, at any time) and perform such obligations on Lessee's behalf and put the same in good order, condition and repair, and the cost, plus five percent (5%) of the cost as an administrative fee, will be paid by Lessee upon demand by Lessor. Lessee shall not, without Lessor's prior written consent, make any alterations or improvements to the Premises. Lessee shall defend, hold harmless and indemnify Lessor against costs or losses (including Lessor's legal fees) arising from any mechanics' or materialmens' lien against the Premises resulting from any alteration of the Premises by Lessee. On the last day of the Term, or on any sooner termination, Lessee shall surrender the Premises to Lessor in the same condition as received, ordinary wear and tear excepted, clean and free of debris.

8. Insurance; Indemnity. Lessee shall, at Lessee's expense, obtain and keep in force during the term of this Lease a policy of commercial general liability insurance, issued by an insurance company acceptable to Lessor, insuring Lessor and Lessee against any liability, damages, cost or expense arising out of the ownership, use, occupancy or maintenance of the Premises. Such insurance shall be a combined single limit policy in an amount not less than $500,000 per occurrence and $2,000,000 in the general aggregate. The policy shall insure performance by Lessee of the indemnity provisions of this Section 8. The limits of said insurance shall not, however, limit the liability of Lessee under this Lease. Lessor, and its mortgagees will be named as additional insureds under these policies. Lessee agrees that such limits may be reasonably increased by notice from Lessor from time to time. Lessee will deliver to Lessor copies of policies of such insurance or certificates evidencing the existence and amounts of such insurance with loss payable clauses as required by this Section 8. These policies must not be cancelable or subject to reduction of coverage or other modification except after thirty (30) days' prior written notice to Lessor. Lessee shall, at least thirty (30) days prior to the expiration of such policies, furnish Lessor with renewals or binders thereof, or Lessor may order such insurance and charge the cost, plus five percent (5%) of the cost as an administrative fee, to Lessee, which amount Lessee agrees to pay immediately to Lessor upon Lessor's demand.

Lessee will indemnify, defend and hold Lessor, its agents, representatives, officers, directors and shareholders harmless from and against any and all claims, demands, liabilities, judgments, costs, expenses, suits and investigations arising from Lessee's use or occupancy of the Premises, or from the conduct of Lessee's business or from any activity, work or things done, permitted or suffered by Lessee in or about the Premises or elsewhere and shall further indemnify, defend and hold Lessor, its agents, representatives, officers, directors and shareholders harmless from and against any and all claims, demands, liabilities, judgments, costs, expenses, suits and investigations arising from any breach or default in the performance of any obligation on Lessee's part to be performed under the terms of this Lease or of any representation or warranty made by Lessee in this Lease, or arising from any negligence, act or omission of Lessee, or any of Lessee's agents, contractors, or employees, and from and against all costs, attorneys' fees, expenses and liabilities incurred in the defense of any such claim, suit, investigation, action or proceeding brought hereon. The defense of any action, claim, suit, investigation or proceeding against Lessor or the Premises shall be at Lessee's sole cost and expense and shall be undertaken by counsel satisfactory to Lessor. Lessee, as a material part of the consideration to Lessor, hereby assumes all risk of damage to property or injury to persons, in, upon or about the Premises arising from any cause and Lessee hereby waives all claims in respect thereof against Lessor.

Lessee hereby agrees that Lessor shall not be liable for injury to Lessee's business or any loss of income or for damage to the goods, wares, equipment, machinery, trade fixtures, merchandise or other property of Lessee, Lessee's employees, invitees, customers, or any other person in or about the Premises, nor shall Lessor be liable for injury to the person of Lessee, Lessee's employees, agents or contractors.

9. <u>Damage or Destruction.</u> For purposes of this Section, "Partial Damage" means damage to the Premises to the extent of 30% or less of the Premises, as determined by Lessor, and "Destruction" means damage to the Premises of greater than 30% of the Premises, as determined by Lessor. In the event any damage to the Premises shall occur, Lessee shall provide immediate notice thereof to Lessor and such damage shall be dealt with as follows:

(i) If the Premises shall suffer Partial Damage by fire or other cause that is not due to the fault or neglect of Lessee, Lessee's agents, contractors, or employees, as determined by Lessor, Lessor shall repair the damage at Lessor's expense and the Base Rent until the repairs are made shall be apportioned by Lessor according to the Premises portion that is usable by Lessee. With respect to pre-paid Base Rent, Lessor shall calculate the amount of Base Rent attributable to the unusable portion of the Premises according to the number of days such portion remains unusable and shall refund such amount to Lessee. With respect to Base Rent paid in monthly installments, Lessor shall abate Base Rent using the same calculation method.

(ii) If the Premises shall suffer Partial Damage by fire or other cause that is due to the fault or neglect of Lessee or Lessee's agents, contractors or employees, as determined by Lessor and without prejudice to any other rights or remedies of Lessor and without prejudice to the rights of subrogation of Lessor's insurer, Lessor shall repair the damage at Lessor's expense, but there shall be no refund or abatement of Base Rent.

(iii) If Destruction of the Premises occurs or, in Lessor's judgment, otherwise renders the Premises untenantable, Lessor may, but shall not be required to, within ninety (90) days after the Destruction, give Lessee a notice that the Lease is terminated on the third day after the date the notice is given, and Lessee shall vacate and surrender the Premises to Lessor. If Lessee shall not be in default under this Lease and the Destruction shall have not been due to the fault or neglect of Lessee or Lessee's agents, contractors or employees, as determined by Lessor, Lessee's liability for Base Rent shall cease as of the day following the date of the Destruction and, if applicable, Lessor shall refund the remainder of the Base Rent pre-paid for the Term.

Lessee hereby expressly waives the provisions of Section 227 of the Real Property Law of the State of New York and agrees that this Section 9 shall govern and control in lieu thereof. If the Partial Damage or Destruction be due to the fault or neglect of Lessee or Lessee's agents, contractors or employees, the debris shall be removed by Lessee at Lessee's sole expense.

10. Real Property Taxes. Lessee will pay all Real Property Taxes incurred by Lessor with respect to the Premises during the Term. "Real Property Taxes" means any form of real estate tax or assessment, general, special, supplemental, ordinary or extraordinary, and any license fee, commercial rental tax, improvement bond or bonds, levy or tax (other than inheritance, personal income or estate taxes) imposed on Lessor with respect to the Premises or on the Premises itself or that relates to the tenancy of Lessee by any governmental authority. If the Premises are not separately assessed, Lessee's liability shall be an equitable proportion of the Real Property Taxes for all of the land and improvements included within the tax parcel assessed, such proportion to be determined by Lessor from the respective valuations assigned in the assessor's work sheets or such other information as may be reasonably available. Lessor's reasonable determination thereof in good-faith, shall be conclusive.

11. Utilities. Lessee shall pay for all water, gas, heat, light, garbage disposal, sewer, power, telephone and other utilities and services supplied to the Premises, together with any taxes thereon. If any such services are not separately metered to Lessee, Lessee shall pay a reasonable proportion to be determined by Lessor of all charges jointly metered with other Premises.

12. Assignment and Subletting. Lessee shall not voluntarily or by operation of law assign, transfer, hypothecate, pledge, mortgage, sublet, or otherwise transfer or encumber all or any part of Lessee's interest in this Lease or in the Premises without Lessor's prior written consent. Any attempted assignment, transfer, hypothecation, pledge, mortgage, encumbrance or subletting shall be void, and shall constitute a material default under this Lease. The transfer of substantially all of the assets of Lessee or fifty percent (50%) or more of the stock, partnership interests or membership interests in Lessee (or, if Lessee is a limited partnership, the corporate general partner, if any of such limited partnership), whether direct or indirect or in one or more transactions, shall be deemed to be an assignment. Lessor shall be permitted to assign this Lease and all of its rights and obligations under this Lease at any time and to any individual or entity.

13. Defaults; Remedies.

13.1. Defaults. The occurrence of any one or more of the following events shall constitute a material default and breach of this Lease by Lessee (an "Event of Default"):

(i) The vacating or abandonment of the Premises by Lessee;

(ii) The failure by Lessee to make any payment of Base Rent, Additional Rent or any other monetary obligation required to be paid by Lessee hereunder, as and when due, where such amount is delivered by mail and not postmarked on or prior to the fifteenth (15th) day after which such payment is due or delivered otherwise more than fifteen (15) days after such payment is due; or

(iii) The failure by Lessee to observe or perform any of the covenants, conditions or provisions of this Lease to be observed or performed by Lessee, where such failure shall continue for a period of fifteen (15) days after written notice thereof from Lessor to Lessee.

(iv) (a) The making by Lessee of any general arrangement of assignment for the benefit of creditors; (b) Lessee becomes a "debtor" as defined in 11 U.S.C. § 1101 or any successor statute thereto (unless, in the case of a petition filed against Lessee, the same is dismissed within thirty (30) days); (c) the appointment of a trustee or receiver to take possession of substantially all of Lessee's assets located at the Premises or of Lessee's interest in this Lease, where possession is not restored to Lessee within thirty (30) days; or (d) the attachment, execution or other judicial seizure of substantially all of Lessee's assets located at the Premises or of Lessee's interest in this Lease, where such seizure is not discharged and reversed within thirty (30) days.

(v) The breach of any representation or warranty made by Lessee.

13.2. <u>Remedies.</u> In the event of an Event of Default, Lessor may, at any time thereafter, with or without notice or demand and without limiting Lessor in the exercise of any right or remedy, which Lessor may have by reason of such Event of Default:

(i) Terminate Lessee's right to possession of the Premises by any lawful means, in which case this Lease shall terminate and Lessee shall immediately surrender possession of the Premises to Lessor in the manner set forth above. In such event, Lessor shall be entitled to recover from Lessee all damages incurred by Lessor by reason of such Event of Default including, but not limited to, the cost of recovering possession of the Premises; expenses of reletting, including necessary renovation, cleaning and alteration of the Premises, reasonable attorneys' fees.

(ii) Maintain Lessee's right to possession in which case this Lease shall continue in effect whether or not Lessee shall have abandoned the Premises. In such event, Lessor shall be entitled to enforce all of Lessor's rights and remedies under this Lease, including the right to recover Base Rent and other charges under this Lease as they become due hereunder. Lessor shall not be bound by any duty to mitigate against such abandonment.

(iii) Pursue any other remedy now or hereafter available to Lessor under the law or judicial decisions of the state wherein the Premises are located. Unpaid installments of Base Rent and Additional Rent and other unpaid monetary obligations of Lessee under the terms of this Lease shall bear interest from the date due at the maximum rate then allowable by law.

(iv) Re-enter the Premises at its option without declaring the Lease term ended, and re-let the whole or any part thereof for the account of Lessee, on such terms and conditions and at such rent as Lessor may deem proper, collecting such rent and applying it to the amounts due from Lessee hereunder and to the expense of such re-letting and to any other damage or expense so sustained by Lessor, or to any such item or items, recovering from Lessee the difference between the proceeds of such re-letting and the amount of the rentals reserved hereunder, and any such damage or expense from time to time, which said sum Lessee agrees to pay upon demand. Lessor shall not, by any re-entry or other act, be deemed to have terminated this Lease or the liability of Lessee for the total rent hereunder, or any installment thereof then due or thereafter accruing, or for damages, unless Lessor shall notify Lessee, in writing, that Lessor has so elected to terminate the Lease.

14. Condemnation. If the Premises or any portion thereof are taken under the power of eminent domain, this Lease shall terminate on the date when title vests pursuant to such taking. The Base Rent shall be apportioned as of such date, and any Base Rent paid for any period beyond such date shall be repaid to Lessee. Lessee shall not be entitled to any part of the award for such taking or any payment in lieu thereof, and Lessee hereby assigns and transfers to Lessor any claim it may have to compensation for damages as a result of any condemnation.

15. Attorney's Fees. Upon demand of Lessor, Lessee shall pay all Lessor's attorney's fees related to the enforcement of the terms and conditions of this Lease against Lessee.

16. Estoppel Certificate; Attornment; Subordination. Lessee shall at any time upon not less than ten (10) days' prior written notice from Lessor execute, acknowledge and deliver to Lessor a statement in writing (i) certifying that this Lease is unmodified and in full force and effect (or, if modified, stating the nature of such modification and certifying that this Lease, as so modified, is in full force and effect) and the date to which the Base Rent, Additional Rent and other charges are paid in advance, if any, and (ii) acknowledging that there are not, to Lessee's best knowledge, any uncured defaults on the part of Lessor hereunder, or specifying such defaults if any are claimed. Any such statement may be conclusively relied upon by any prospective purchaser or mortgagee of the Premises. Lessee shall, in the event any proceedings are brought or any power of sale is exercised for the foreclosure of any mortgage encumbering any interest in the Premises, if so requested by the purchaser at such foreclosure sale, attorn to the purchaser upon such foreclosure or sale, and recognize such purchaser as the Lessor under this Lease. For purposes hereof, acceptance of a deed in lieu of foreclosure shall be deemed to be a purchase at a foreclosure sale. This Lease, at Lessor's option, shall be subordinate to any ground lease, mortgage, deed of trust, or any other hypothecation or security now or hereafter placed upon the real property of which the Premises are a part and to any and all advances made on the security thereof and to renewals, modifications, consolidations, replacements and extensions thereof. Lessee agrees to execute any documents required to effectuate an attornment, a subordination or to make this Lease prior to the lien of any mortgage, deed of trust or ground lease, as the case may be, within 10 days of receiving any of these documents.

   17. Severability. The invalidity of any provision of this Lease as determined by a court of competent jurisdiction, shall in no way affect the validity of any other provision.

   18. Late Charge on Past-due Obligations. If any installment of Base Rent, Additional Rent or any other sum due from Lessee is not received by Lessor within ten (10) days after it is due, then, without any requirement for notice to Lessee, Lessee will immediately pay to Lessor a late charge of One Hundred Dollars ($100). Acceptance of such late charge by Lessor shall in no event constitute a waiver of Lessee's default with respect to such overdue amount, nor prevent Lessor from exercising any of the other rights and remedies granted hereunder.

   19. Time of Essence. Time is of the essence with respect to Lessee's obligations to be performed under this Lease.

   20. Incorporation of Prior Agreements; Amendments. This Lease contains all agreements of the parties with respect to the subject matter of this Lease and supersedes all prior agreements or understandings pertaining to these matters. Any amendment to this Lease must be in a writing signed by Lessor and Lessee.

   21. Notices. All notices, requests and demands to be made hereunder to the parties hereto shall be in writing and shall be delivered by hand, by overnight courier or sent by registered or certified mail (postage prepaid) through the United States Postal Service to the addresses shown below or such other addresses which the parties may provide to one another in accordance herewith. Such notices, requests and demands, if sent by mail, shall be deemed given five (5) days after deposit in the United States mail; if delivered by hand, shall be deemed given when delivered; and if sent by overnight courier, shall be deemed given one (1) day after deposit with such overnight courier.

LESSOR: Learned Landlord, Inc.

                     PO Box 3252

                     Nowhere City, NY 00010

Attention: Learned Landlord

LESSEE: Sam Seller

                     1629 Main Street

                     Smalltown, NY 00013

22. <u>Waivers.</u> No waiver by Lessor of any provision hereof shall be deemed a waiver of any other provision hereof or of any subsequent breach by Lessee of the same or any other provision. No attempt by Lessee to cause an accord and satisfaction to exist by any statement on any check or other document will be effective, and Lessor may accept any payment without any effect on its rights against Lessee.

23. <u>Holding Over.</u> If Lessee holds over after the expiration or earlier termination of the term hereof without the express written consent of Lessor, Lessee shall become a tenant at sufferance only, at an annual Base Rent equal to one hundred fifty percent (150%) of the Base Rent in effect upon the date of such expiration, prorated on a daily basis and otherwise upon the terms and conditions herein specified, so far as applicable. Acceptance by Lessor of Base Rent after such expiration or earlier termination shall not result in a renewal or extension of the Lease except to the extent provided in this Section 23. The foregoing provisions of this Section 23 are in addition to and do not affect Lessor's rights of reentry or any other rights of Lessor hereunder or as otherwise provided by law and do not give to Lessee any right to hold over after the expiration or earlier termination of the term thereof.

24. <u>Cumulative Remedies.</u> No remedy or election hereunder shall be deemed exclusive but shall, wherever possible, be cumulative with all other remedies at law or in equity.

25. <u>Covenants and Conditions.</u> Each provision of this Lease performable by Lessee shall be deemed to be both a covenant and a condition.

26. <u>Binding Effect; Choice of Law.</u> This Lease shall bind the parties, their personal representatives, successors and permitted assigns. This Lease shall be governed by the laws of the State of New York, without giving effect to any conflicts-of-laws principles.

27. <u>Lessor's Access.</u> Lessor and Lessor's agents shall have the right to enter the Premises at reasonable times for the purpose of inspecting the same, showing the same to prospective purchasers, lenders, or lessees, and making such alterations, repairs, improvements or additions to the Premises or to the building of which they are a part as Lessor may deem necessary or desirable. Lessor may at any time place on or about the Premises any ordinary "For Sale" signs and Lessor may at any time during the last one hundred eighty (180) days of the term hereof place on or about the Premises any ordinary "For Lease" signs, all without rebate of rent or liability to Lessee.

28. <u>Consents.</u> Unless expressly stated otherwise, if the Lessor is required to take any action under this Lease by written consent, the granting of any such consent shall be in Lessor's absolute and sole discretion.

29. <u>Authority.</u> Lessee hereby represents and warrants to Lessor the following:

(a) Lessee is a duly formed, validly existing corporation in good standing of the State of New York; and

(b) If Lessee is a corporation, trust, general or limited partnership or limited liability company, each individual executing this Lease on behalf of such entity represents and warrants that he or she is duly authorized to execute and deliver this Lease on behalf of said entity. At the request of Lessor, if Lessee is a corporation, trust or partnership, Lessee shall, within thirty (30) days after execution of this Lease, deliver to Lessor evidence of such authority satisfactory to Lessor.

30. <u>Lender's Requirements.</u> Lessee hereby agrees to make any reasonable changes to this Lease which may be required in good faith by a bona fide lender in connection with the financing of the real property of which the Premises are a part, provided that such changes do not materially interfere with Lessee's use of the Premises or increase the Base Rent or other costs of Lessee's use and occupancy of the Premises.

31. <u>Hazardous Materials.</u> Lessee agrees not to use, treat, sell, store, generate, manufacture, emit, transport or dispose of and not to suffer or permit anyone else to use, treat, store, generate, manufacture, emit, transport or dispose of, whether temporarily or permanently, any hazardous material, whether in the form of toxic substances, pollutants, waste or otherwise at, on, or beneath the Premises. At all times during the Term, Lessee shall promptly submit to Lessor any notices it receives from any governmental entity in connection with a violation or alleged violation of any environmental laws, regulations or orders or Lessee's use, treatments, storage, manufacture, generation, sale, emission, transportation or disposal of hazardous materials.

IN WITNESS WHEREOF, the parties hereto have executed this Lease on the date first above written.

Learned Lessor, Inc.

By:_____
    "LESSOR"

Sam Seller

By: *Sam Seller*
    "LESSEE"

Exhibit A – Legal Description [omitted from the problem]

Chapter 11
DETERMINING CONTRACT TERMS WITH UCC § 2-207

PREVIEW

In this Chapter, we will look at a "battle of the forms" problem, a common kind of problem in a modern world of mass-produced forms. The problem comes to you after the parties have terminated their contract, disagreeing in the first instance about who is to blame for the problem. Such an outcome represents a failure of the contract and of the parties (and their lawyers) to work things out in a less expensive and, therefore, more efficient way. Having failed to work things out, your client is facing a lawsuit for failing to pay for delivered fabric, which your client contends is defective. Your client has suffered its own losses because it incorporated the defective goods into its own products that were, in turn, defective. Your job will be to determine what the client's legal position is in this controversy.

SUBSTANTIVE CONTENT:

- UCC § 2-207
- Consequential damages

SKILLS AND VALUES UTILIZED:

- Read and analyze documents
- Determine what terms in the documents are relevant
- Apply § 2-207 to determine the likely terms in the document

ESTIMATED TIME FOR COMPLETION: 60 Minutes

LEVEL OF DIFFICULTY (1 to 5):

EXERCISE K:

After law school, a small law firm hired you and you are anxious to bring new clients to the firm. A friend referred Pat Stuart, the president of Dolphin Corporation, to you. Pat came to see you today to discuss a problem the company has with one of its major fabric suppliers, Delilah Corporation. During the interview with Pat, you discovered the following facts.

Dolphin Corporation, purchases fabric and uses it to produce prosthetic liners for amputees to wear under prosthetic devices (such as artificial legs, arms, and hands) for the limb that has been amputated. Prosthetic liners cover the residual limb of an amputee before the prosthetic is fitted over the limb and permit the prosthetic device to fit more snugly over the amputated limb. The comfort of these liners is paramount to Dolphin's customers because it makes a difference in their ability to use their prosthetic device without discomfort.

After trying material from a number of different companies and conducting a series of tests, Dolphin determined that the fabric from Delilah best suited its needs. The material produced by Delilah through a special manufacturing process was a high tech fabric that was soft, easily stretched, very pliable, and quite strong. It appeared to be a big improvement over the last fabric Dolphin used to make these liners.

Pat told you that, at first, she was very pleased with the fabric and Dolphin's customers praised the comfort of the liners made from the Delilah fabric. Delilah made four deliveries using the same purchase order system without any problems between the two companies. After a few months, however, Dolphin started receiving complaints from customers about inconsistencies with the liners produced from the Delilah fabric. These inconsistencies caused considerable discomfort for customers and the number of complaints increased every week. Consequently, Dolphin began to lose a substantial amount of business. Pat told you that one of her biggest concerns is the amount of business her company has lost. She worked hard to build up her reputation in the industry and it is now in the process of being destroyed.

Pat recently learned that Delilah ran out of one of the components that it used to produce the high tech fabric that it was selling to Dolphin, so it substituted a different component in the yarn but did not notify Dolphin of the substitution. Because of the substitution, the fabric produced by Delilah was not nearly as comfortable as the previous product. The complaints grew more numerous and, due to all of the complaints, Dolphin eventually recalled and destroyed all of the liners that had been made with the substituted fabric provided by Delilah. Pat tells you that they have lost quite a bit of business (and probably business reputation) due to all of the problems with the liners.

Pat also said that, reading between the lines during a conversation with Erin Head, the president of Delilah, Pat came to believe that the reason the fabric may have been problematic was because of the substituted component in the fabric. When Pat confronted Erin about this directly, he attempted to blame the problem on Dolphin's manufacturing process. This bothered Pat so much that she has refused to authorize payment for the remaining Delilah bills and she terminated the relationship with Delilah. She has recently contracted with another company for what she hopes will be a comparable fabric, although it will cost almost 15% more than the other fabric. She is content to pay more for the fabric from this distributor because it is a higher quality than Delilah's fabric. Pat told you that she thinks Delilah should — at a minimum — reimburse her for the material that Dolphin had to discard.

Further, she told you that her company has lost a significant amount of business and she wants to know if Dolphin brought a lawsuit against Delilah, what the chances would be of holding Delilah responsible for the lost business and harm to the company's reputation. She is sufficiently upset about Delilah's refusal to stand by its product that " legal fees will be no object" if she has a viable claim. You told her that trying to quantify the cost of the company's *lost reputation* likely would be quite difficult and extremely expensive and it was probably not worth taking that issue to litigation.

Delilah has continued to bill Dolphin for the fabric that resulted in Dolphin's recall and Pat, of course, will not authorize payment. Delilah, in response, has been making a lot of noise about suing Dolphin unless they are paid immediately.

Pat, as Dolphin's representative, without contacting an attorney, sent a letter notifying Delilah of the problems with the fabric. This letter told Delilah that they needed to provide a consistent comfortable product if they wanted to continue a beneficial long-term relationship. When she received no response, she sent another letter demanding that someone call her to talk about this problem. Pat wants to know whether she should pay for the delivered (but useless) fabric.

Pat gave you a very skimpy file that contained 5 documents: the two letters she sent to Delilah when they began having problems with the material, a letter from Delilah, the purchase order form Pat used to buy the material, and the acknowledgement form Delilah sent back to her. Those documents are reprinted below.

March 1, 0000

James Johnson
Delilah Fabrics, Inc.
222 West Outback Road
Wallabie, TX

Dear Mr. Johnson:

We have begun receiving complaints about the prosthetic liners that we make from your fabric and sell to amputees. Those complaints are directly related to the consistency, or lack thereof, in the fabric we buy from you that we incorporate into our prosthetic liners.

We need to receive a consistent product from you if we're going to continue our mutually beneficial relationship. Please advise us of the steps you plan to take to correct these problems and provide more consistent quality control.

Sincerely,

Pat Stuart

April 1, 0000

James Johnson
Delilah Fabrics, Inc.
222 West Outback Road
Wallabie, TX

Dear Mr. Johnson:

We still have received no response from you about the complaints concerning the prosthetic liners that we make from your fabric and sell to amputees. The complaints continue and we would very much like to receive a response from you in the near future.

As we said in our last letter, we need to receive a consistent product from you if we're going to continue our relationship. Please contact me so we can discuss this matter.

Sincerely,

Pat Stuart

April 15, 0000

Pat Stuart
Dolphin Corporation
Pleasantville
Anywhere, USA 007007

Dear Ms. Stuart

Thank you for your letter of April 1, 0000. I am sorry I have not had the opportunity to contact you sooner but I have been out of the country on business and only just returned this week. I appreciate the problems that you are having with your products but we do not believe that the fabric you have been receiving from us is the cause of the complaints from your customers. Delilah provides an excellent product and none of our other customers seem to be having similar problems. I suggest that you look at your manufacturing process for the problems. If I can be of any other assistance, please do not hesitate to contact me.

Sincerely,

James Johnson
CEO, Delilah Fabrics
222 West Outback Road
Wallabie, Texas 445566

DOLPHIN ORDER FORM

Dear Delilah,

We were quite pleased to make your acquaintance at the recent trade show in Materialville. Your new fabric, 456 Eagle Cloth, with its properties of elasticity, softness, and comfort is exactly what we have been looking for to enhance our products. I am sure that our customers will be very happy with our products made from Eagle Cloth. I am enclosing a shipping requisition for your immediate approval. We would like to receive the cloth as soon as possible, so we can start using the Eagle Cloth in our products. Please feel free to contact me if you have any questions.

SHIPPING INFORMATION:

Company:	Dolphin Corporation
Contact Person:	Athena Schmidt
Tel. No:	600-000-0001

Extension:	9696
Fax. No:	600-000-0002
Address:	234 Pleasant Drive
City:	Pleasantville
State:	Anywhere
Country:	USA
Zip:	007007
E-Mail:	Aschmidt@dolphin.corp.net

BILLING INFORMATION :

Same as Shipping Information

PRODUCTS ORDERED

Item :	456 Eagle cloth
Description :	Multi-colored
Quantity :	500 yards

PAYMENT OPTIONS:

Per our conversation and credit approval we agree to pay within 30 days of receipt with a 1% charge if our payment is late by more than 5 days.

SHIPPING INSTRUCTIONS:

Please ship by:	Shark's Freight Co.
Our Account Number:	6666666

FOB Delilah Corp.

Shark's to pick up on 3 days call

Shark's Tel. No.:	600-888-0000
Contact at Shark's:	Billy Bob Container
Shark's e-mail:	Nelliebell@shark.freight.net

Remedies:

The laws of the state of Anywhere apply to this contract. Buyer refuses to submit to arbitration.

Quality:

Buyer expects quality merchandise and in the event it is not, we reserve the right to terminate any contract we have with your company.

The Delilah form reads as follows:

ACKNOWLEDGEMENT

Delilah Company is pleased to accept your order and will send you the Eagle Cloth material as quickly as possible. We are delighted to have you as our customer.

This acknowledgment shows our willingness to sell to you but please note our requirements on this counter offer.

All goods manufactured by Delilah are guaranteed to be free from defects for 90 days in material and workmanship. There is no implied warranty of merchantability and no other warranty express or implied, unless it is expressly set forth herein.

This agreement is the complete agreement of the parties. No other promises or agreements are made between the parties.

Risk of Loss: The seller will be responsible for delivering the fabric to the buyer's designated freight company. Once the goods are delivered all risk of loss is on the buyer and the buyer is responsible for insuring the goods once they are delivered to the freight company.

BUYER SHALL NOT IN ANY EVENT BE ENTITLED TO, AND SELLER SHALL NOT BE LIABLE FOR INDIRECT OR CONSEQUENTIAL DAMAGES OF ANY NATURE, INCLUDING, WITHOUT BEING LIMITED TO, LOSS OF PROFIT, PROMOTIONAL OR MANUFACTURING EXPENSES, INJURY TO REPUTATION OR LOSS OF CUSTOMERS.

Task One:

Review the facts and the documents in the file that Pat gave you to see whether they tend to establish her legal position, one way or the other, in this situation. Write a couple of short paragraphs delineating (1) what Pat's main objectives are in dealing with this conflict (For example, does she want to keep the contract going? Work out a resolution? Etc.) and (2) what portions of the documents, if any, are *relevant* to this inquiry. When writing the answer to (2) be sure to include clauses of the documents that may undercut her position as well as the clauses that are consistent with her position.

After writing the paragraphs, consult the Self-Assessment 1 for Exercise K on the LexisNexis webcourse.

———————————

Recall that Pat told you, in addition to not paying for the defective fabric, she wants to receive compensation for the injury to her company's reputation (which you said was too expensive to litigate) and the loss of business caused by the defective liners. Assume that Dolphin and Delilah agree that the fabric deviated from the sample supplied and that, therefore, Delilah breached the contract. In this next task, concentrate on Dolphin's desire to obtain consequential damages from Delilah and, for this task, assume that she will be able to quantify and prove lost business as a result of Delilah's breach.

If Delilah breached the contract, as they seem to agree that they did, then on the assumption that the fabric was worthless to Dolphin, Dolphin will be excused from paying. Moreover, if Dolphin can successfully bring a claim for consequential damages, it should obtain some compensation for its damages from Delilah. Thus, having reviewed the forms that were exchanged, you realize the central inquiry is whether the disclaimer of consequential damages in Dolphin's acknowledgment form will hold. You know that (as always) it is important to determine what law will apply to this transaction; however, you have concluded that the UCC should apply because the subject matter of the contract is movable goods[1] and that the applicable State law has the standard UCC language.[2]

You have turned your office upside-down looking for those old Contracts notes before you remembered you burned them, with many of your books, at the picnic that followed the last exam in your first year. So, instead, you turned to the authorities, which revealed that the applicable statute is UCC § 2-207.

Task Two:

Review UCC § 2-207, set out below, and determine what issues will need to be addressed on the question whether consequential damages will be recoverable. Make a list of the issues that you believe will need to be resolved if this goes to court. After you have written your answer, consult Self-Assessment 2 for Exercise K on the LexisNexis web course.[3]

---

[1] **Sidebar**: Applicability of the UCC

Article 2 of the Uniform Commercial Code only applies to transactions in goods. The two relevant sections are 2-102 and 2-103 (k). 2-102 states in part"[u]nless the context otherwise requires, this Article applies to transactions in goods;. ......" And 2-103 (k) provides in part "[g]oods" means all things that are movable at the time of identification to a contract for sale. ...." Since fabric is movable, it is a good. Thus UCC Article 2 applies.

[2] **Sidebar**: UCC State-To-State Deviation.

While it tends to be "uniform," the Uniform Commercial Code is enacted by each State legislature and these lawmakers sometimes change the language of given sections for various reasons. It is always critically important to check the local enactment for alterations from the uniform text.

[3] **Sidebar: Some In's and Out's Of UCC § 2-207**

Since Delilah's form "accepted" Dolphin's order (Acknowledgment, first line), an issue that is *unlikely* to be present here is *whether* the second form was an "acceptance" (the first of the two alternatives in the first line of subsection 1) or something else. This matters for several reasons. If it were *not* an "acceptance" under 2-207 (1), then Dolphin will have a contract only if there is conduct that shows the parties thought they had a contract. That would certainly be true in this case because Delilah and Dolphin have been buying and selling the fabric for some time. If the contract were formed by conduct alone then 2-207 (3) would apply instead of 2-207 (1) and 2-207 (2).

This is important in some cases (though likely not here) because 2-207 (3) and 2-207 (2) do not deal with different and additional terms in the same way. Under 2-207 (3) the so-called "knock out" rule applies. This means that all different and additional terms "knock" one another out the default rules of the UCC will fill the gaps. Since the UCC's default rule permits consequential damages, if Delilah's disclaimer here were "knocked out," the UCC would fill the gaps and Dolphin could claim consequential damages.

§ 2-207. Additional Terms in Acceptance or Confirmation.

(1) A definite and seasonable expression of acceptance or a written confirmation which is sent within a reasonable time operates as an acceptance even though it states terms additional to or different from those offered or agreed upon, unless acceptance is expressly made conditional on assent to the additional or different terms.

(2) The additional terms are to be construed as proposals for addition to the contract. Between merchants such terms become part of the contract unless:

   (a) the offer expressly limits acceptance to the terms of the offer;

   (b) they materially alter it; or

   (c) notification of objection to them has already been given or is given within a reasonable time after notice of them is received.

(3) Conduct by both parties which recognizes the existence of a contract is sufficient to establish a contract for sale although the writings of the parties do not otherwise establish a contract. In such case the terms of the particular contract consist of those terms on which the writings of the parties agree, together with any supplementary terms incorporated under any other provisions of this Act.

From the Official Comments (it is worth reading all of them if your Statutory Supplement contains them):

3. Whether or not additional or different terms will become part of the agreement depends upon the provisions of subsection (2). If they are such as materially to alter the original bargain, they will not be included unless expressly agreed to by the other party. If, however, they are terms which would not so change the bargain they will be incorporated unless notice of objection to them has already been given or is given within a reasonable time.

4. Examples of typical clauses which would normally "materially alter" the contract and so result in surprise or hardship if incorporated without express awareness by the other party are: a clause negating such standard warranties as that of merchantability or fitness for a particular purposes in circumstances in which either warranty normally attaches; a clause requiring a guaranty of 90% or 100% deliveries in a case such as contract by cannery, where the usage of the trade allows greater quantity leeways; a clause reserving to the seller the power to cancel upon the buyer's failure to meet any invoice when due; a clause requiring that complaints be made in a time materially shorter than customary or reasonable.

Task Three:

Although it is highly unlikely that a court would apply the common law instead of the UCC, would it make any difference? (Even though it is very unlikely, one never knows what opposing counsel might argue to try to win the case). Write a few sentences explaining your answer. After you have written your answer, Self-Assessment 3 for Exercise K on the LexisNexis web course.

Task Four:

Assuming that you can make a good argument to delete the consequential damages disclaimer, you still will need to be able to recover and prove consequential damages. Read UCC 2-715 (2) and determine what facts you will need to find out from your client to be successful on a consequential damages claim. Make a list of the facts you need. After you have written your list, consult Self-Assessment 4 for Exercise K on the LexisNexis web course.

§ 2-715. Buyer's Incidental and Consequential Damages.

(2) Consequential damages resulting from the seller's breach include

(a) any loss resulting from general or particular requirements and needs of which the seller at the time of contracting had reason to know and which could not reasonably be prevented by cover or otherwise; . . .

Task Five:

1. Go to the LexisNexis web course and take the short Review Test on this material.

2. Then go to Lexis.com and bring up *Paul Gottlieb & Co. Inc. v. Alps South Corp.*, 985 So. 2d 1. You can do this by clicking the Get a Document tab at the top and then pasting or typing the citation into the box. Please read the case (you should be able to do this quickly since you've already read much of it and there is no need to brief it). The discussion that relates to much of our problem begins on page 7 of the opinion.

Chapter 12
INTER-CLIENT CONFLICTS OF INTEREST

PREVIEW

The very nature of legal representation makes it difficult for a lawyer to bring the vigor of full representation to two clients whose interests are in conflict. But, given our increasingly interconnected world, it is inevitable that, on occasion, the interests of a lawyer's potential client will conflict to a greater or lesser extent with those of a pre-existing client. Since most lawyers are loath to turn down paying work, when potential work is available that might present problems the natural tendency is to find ways to reconcile a conflict so that both clients can be represented. The Model Rules of Professional Conduct allow lawyers, in some settings, to represent two clients whose interests conflict, provided that the lawyer obtain the "informed consent" to the, perhaps, less-than-optimal representation of both clients. In other cases, the Rules prohibit representation even with the informed consent of both clients.

Lawyer conflict of interest problems are pervasive in law practice and are sometimes particularly difficult in non-litigation work. When clients are litigating, it is quite obvious that a lawyer should not be able to represent both antagonists at the same time. (The idea of a courtroom lawyer objecting to her own questions may even have comedic possibilities). In non-litigation work, the problems are not as easy to see. What could be wrong if a lawyer is asked to represent both parties, not antagonistic to one another, who simply want to make a contract with one another?

Conflict of interest problems can present severe professional hazards to lawyers who are insensitive to them, ignore them, or attempt to stretch the rules. These problems will be with you regularly in your practice and it is important to begin developing your sensitivity to them now.

In this exercise, we will simply introduce you to lawyer conflict of interest problems in the context of contract negotiation in the corporate setting. This is a vast subject and, in an exercise like this, we can only scratch the surface. Your tasks in this exercise will be 1) to try to understand in two different situations some of the ways the interests of two clients might conflict; 2) read and apply the pertinent Model Rules of Professional Conduct to the situation, 3) draft a form of "Informed Consent" for both clients to sign.

SUBSTANTIVE CONTENT:

- Model Rules of Professional Conduct 1.7(a) and (b) (conflict of interest)
- Model Rule 1.0(e) (informed consent)
- Model Rule 1.6(a) (confidentiality)
- Model Rule 1.2(c) (limiting representation)
- Model Rule 1.5(b) (communication of the fee)

SKILLS AND VALUES UTILIZED:

- Determining who the client is in corporate representation
- Developing sensitivity to conflict of interest problems in different circumstances
- Understanding where the Rules limit conflicting representation even with the consent of both clients
- Drafting an informed consent provision for clients whose interests are in conflict but who are, under the rules, permitted to consent to limited representation

ESTIMATED TIME FOR COMPLETION: 60 Minutes

LEVEL OF DIFFICULTY (1 to 5):

EXERCISE L: Part 1

You graduated from law school several years ago and work in a small law firm. You have represented Jennifer, one of your old college friends, since you became a lawyer. You have done estate planning work for her, represented her in some of her business dealings with others, and even came close to representing her in litigation she was considering against another business, but that litigation never got off the ground. You are very close friends as well and Jennifer seeks your counsel often. Jennifer has been very entrepreneurial since college and is getting rich. Working with a few other people, she has developed a group of new software applications for finance that have really taken off.

With her business booming, Jennifer decided to raise some capital by incorporating. She is now the Chief Executive Officer (she loves the sound of "CEO") of Fanatical Software, Inc., and is a large shareholder. Others who have invested in Fanatical Software as shareholders include some of Jennifer's relatives and friends as well as some strangers who learned about what she was doing and wanted to get in on it. The company now has about 40 employees and continues to grow.

A few months ago Jennifer gave you what she thought was great news. On Jennifer's recommendation, the Board of Directors of Fanatical Software, Inc., decided to hire your law firm as their Outside Counsel to advise the company on the whole range of things on which an up-and-coming business needs advice.

A corporate Board of Directors is clearly in a position to engage outside counsel — a corporate board is responsible for the overall direction and health of a corporation. Corporation law makes the Board of Directors fiduciaries for, and ultimately answerable to, the shareholders; the CEO and other employees are, in turn, ultimately answerable to the Board.

But Boards typically delegate nearly all of the day-to-day decisions to the CEO and to employees answerable to the CEO. In her capacity as CEO Jennifer recommended that Fanatical hire your firm as its outside counsel. Your firm's work for Fanatical Software will probably bring the firm as much as $30,000 to $50,000 a year in fees.

But since Jennifer, the CEO, was a longstanding personal client, representing her company was not a simple proposition: there was a distinct possibility that conflicts of interest would develop.

Introduction to Client Conflicts of Interest in the Corporate Setting:

The law school Professional Responsibility course teaches that a lawyer for a corporation is a lawyer for the company, not for any particular individuals within it. That is to say, if and when you agree to represent Fanatical Software, you agree to represent it as an entity that is different in the eyes of the law and separate from the individuals who work there. Because the Fanatical Software Board (which ultimately speaks for the entity)[1] and Jennifer may not see eye-to-eye on every issue, you had a sense that there might be a conflict of interest despite the fact that Jennifer and the Board were on cordial terms and wanted the same thing. Your simultaneous representation of Fanatical Software and of Jennifer might eventually bring you into a conflict of interest

---

[1] Technically, the members of the Board and the entity itself are also separate and one could run into conflicts problems between the Board and the entity if, for example, the Board breached its duties to its shareholders. This is beyond the scope of our discussion here; we will assume that the potential Board member-entity conflicts have been appropriately managed.

situation, which could violate the ABA Model Rules of Professional Conduct (hereinafter "Model Rules").[2]

The Model Rules have many provisions governing conflicts of interest. Conflicts generally arise because the lawyer owes loyalty, independent judgment, and confidentiality to each of her clients. If two clients have conflicting interests, it is impossible to be fully "loyal" to them, to exercise independent judgment on each of their behalf, or keep their secrets all at once.

Model Rule 1.7(a) defines a "concurrent conflict of interest" to exist if:

1) the representation of one client will be directly adverse to another client; or

2) there is a significant risk that the representation of one or more clients will be materially limited by the lawyer's responsibilities to another client, a former client, or a third person or by a personal interest of the lawyer.

Model Rule 1.7(b) then permits a lawyer to represent both clients provided

1) the lawyer reasonably believes that the lawyer will be able to provide competent and diligent representation to each affected client;

2) the representation is not prohibited by law;

3) the representation does not involve the assertion of a claim by one client against another client represented by the lawyer in the same litigation or other proceeding before a tribunal; and

4) each affected client gives informed consent.

In transactional settings, it is Rules 1.7(b)(1) and (b)(4) that are usually the focus.

An easy way to begin thinking about inter-client conflicts is to focus on the relationships that the clients might have with one another and how they might clash with one another. To take a simple example, one generally could represent two married individuals who come to the lawyer for estate planning - in most cases the individuals' interests will not be in conflict. By contrast, for obvious reasons, one could not represent both if they came to the lawyer to begin a contested divorce case. Representing the two in a "friendly" divorce would be risky. The parties' relationship is a marriage and the dissolution of that marriage puts their interests at odds with one another even in a "friendly" case.[3]

---

[2] The Model Rules of Professional Conduct (in effect, with state-to-state variations in most jurisdictions) have elaborate rules governing lawyers' professional responsibilities to their clients; you will study those rules in detail in upper-class Professional Responsibility courses. This book introduces you to some of them in several of its Chapters.

[3] *See* ROTUNDA, RONALD D., AND JOHN S. DZIENSKOWSK, LEGAL ETHICS – A LAWYERS DESKBOOK ON PROFESSIONAL RESPONSIBILITY CURRENT THROUGH 2009–2010 §1-7-2 (2009).

Experts differ on whether a lawyer *can* represent two spouses in this context and even those who believe it is possible with appropriate consent differ on how advisable it might be.[4]

To identify conflicts of interest, one has to focus on the interests of each client and then see where they might come into conflict. In transactional settings such as this one, one has to imagine the problems that the relationship between the two clients might generate.

Jennifer is, among other things,[5] a very important, and probably well-paid, employee of Fanatical Software.

Task One:

Jot down ways in which Jennifer and the Corporation could come into conflict because one is an employee of the other. After you have written your answer, consult Self-Assessment 1 for Exercise L on the LexisNexis web course.

Informed Consent and Limited Representation:

For now, suffice it to say that the Model Rules' approach to addressing most client conflicts is to 1) identify the kind of conflict or potential conflict involved; 2) ask the lawyer whether she can form a reasonable belief as to whether the lawyer can represent both clients in a competent and diligent manner notwithstanding the conflict; and 3) if so, and if the lawyer still wants to represent both, obtain the informed consent to the representation from each client.[6] In those cases where representation is permissible with "informed consent," the focus often becomes on whether the consent the clients may have given was proper or adequately "informed." If it was not, there is an impermissible conflict in violation of the rules. As you might expect, "informed consent" is defined. Model Rule 1.0(e) provides:

> "Informed consent" denotes the consent by a person to a proposed course of conduct after the lawyer has communicated adequate information and explanation about the material risks of and reasonable available alternatives to a proposed course of conduct.

---

[4] *See* William Statsky, Family Law at pp 33–34 (5th ed. 2002) (stating that multiple representation in dissolutions of marriage may be ethical, but attorney's are urged to avoid multiple representation even when ethically proper).

[5] Jennifer is also a *shareholder* of Fanatical Software. The Board owes duties to, and is ultimately answerable to, the shareholders (your courses on business organizations will focus on what those duties to shareholders are). If the Board has duties to the shareholders, the shareholders have corresponding rights. In our legal system, that usually means that there is some vehicle for shareholders enforcing their rights when the Board violates them (again, courses in corporations and other organizations will teach you how this is done).

Whatever those duties / rights are, and however they are enforced (again, the subject of other courses), it seems clear that representing Jennifer as an investor in any kind of shareholder action against the Board members or the entity that you are also representing (there could be actions against either) would entail a conflict of interest. Jennifer's likelihood of suing the Board as a shareholder, and therefore the likelihood of this particular conflict is very low but it would be useful to identify it and address it at the outset.

[6] Model Rule of Professional Conduct 1.7(b), quoted above.

Many, if not most, lawyer conflict of interest problems arise from the fact that it is in a lawyer's business interest to represent as many clients as possible; lawyers do not like to turn down fee-paying clients. By the same token, two clients might want to pay for one lawyer instead of two, even if the one lawyer might give each a little less than they might get with separate counsel because of the conflict. While some lawyers would conclude that simultaneous representation of both Jennifer and Fanatical Software would be ill-advised and turn down the organizational representation, most probably would not. There is no direct adversity at this point under Model Rule 1.7(a)(1). Would one nonetheless conclude that representation of either Jennifer or Fanatical Software posed a significant risk that the representation could be "materially limited by the lawyer's responsibilities" to the other under Model Rule 1.7(a)(2)? Experts seem to agree that the conflicts endemic in representing both principals and entity in the small corporate setting can be managed.

Lawyers are required to maintain the confidentiality of information relating to a client's representation unless the client gives informed consent to disclosure of that information. Model Rule 1.6(a). If a lawyer represents two clients whose interests potentially conflict and obtains confidential information from each of them that relates to their conflicting interests, she may find herself in a very uncomfortable situation. The law provides that when a lawyer represents two clients in one matter, the confidences of each client cannot be kept from the other.[7] Thus, in our problem, if you generally represented both Jennifer and Fanatical with respect to employment and the question was "what should the negotiated terms of Jennifer's employment contract be," knowledge of Jennifer's "bottom line" or her alternatives to her continued employment with Fanatical would inevitably benefit Fanatical in its negotiations with Jennifer and vice versa. It seems very doubtful that, if this issue (or others related to Jennifer's employment) were to arise, that you would be able to represent either of them without compromising their interests.

While informed consent from both clients might work up to a point in this setting, a better way to resolve this part of the conflict problem might be to limit your representation to exclude, for both clients, all issues related to Jennifer's employment relationship with Fanatical.

The Model Rules permit limited representation provided that the client gives "informed consent." Model Rule 1.2(c). Thus, within the

---

[7] One group of commentators said it this way: "[A]t least absent an express agreement to the contrary, the attorney in such a situation cannot refuse to disclose to one client matters that are material to that client's representation and that are conveyed to the attorney by another client." Thomas L. Browne, Esq., et al., *The Rules of Engagement: An Engagement Letter and Conflicts Waiver Compendium* (available on the LexisNexis web course).

lawyer-client **Engagement Agreement**[8] one might find limits on the scope of representation, information about conflicts of interest for the client to give informed consent, the basis for the lawyer's fee and the client's obligation to pay it, and other matters that will structure the professional[9] relationship between lawyer and client. Here is language that you might use, within your Engagement Agreement with Fanatical, to exclude any representation with respect to Jennifer's employment issues:

> Lawyer and client understand that lawyer's representation will exclude representation of either Jennifer or Fanatical Software on all issues related to Jennifer's employment with Fanatical, including issues related to compensation, benefits, performance, continuation of employment, severance, and the like. If client requires representation on such issues, it / she will obtain separate counsel.

You would want to limit your representation of Jennifer in the same way.[10] If you would like to see a full-blown Engagement Agreement for a situation similar to this one, drafted by an excellent lawyer, please look on the LexisNexis web course for this Chapter.

EXERCISE L: Part 2

You excluded employment matters from your representation of both clients. The representation of both Jennifer and Fanatical Software has proceeded smoothly, but it has required a measure of vigilance on

---

[8] While there is no specific requirement in the Rules, sound practice demands an "Engagement Agreement" at the commencement of representation so that both lawyer and client understand the scope and limits of the lawyer's representation. The Rules do envision a writing at the start of representation, however: Model Rule 1.5(b) requires that the lawyer communicate "the basis or rate of the fee" to a new client, "preferably in writing" "before or within a reasonable time after commencing the representation." Some states made the writing mandatory and it is certainly the better practice.

[9] The lawyer-client relationship is clearly "contractual" but it is much more than that. The law has come to analyze lawyer-client problems using analysis that begins with contract principles but adds in other considerations arising from the special nature of this particular relationship. The contract analysis is sufficiently nuanced and overlaid with other considerations that it merits its own courses in the law school curriculum, and indexing in the legal cataloging system. While we refer to it as a "professional relationship," you can expect many of the rules will show strong traces of contract law.

[10] While limiting the scope of your representation to exclude issues related to Jennifer's employment with Fanatical solves some of the employment-related conflict problem, it doesn't solve all of it. Consider the confidential information that each of the clients might divulge to you, with respect to their respective interests, about employment questions generally. Suppose, for example, Fanatical was considering a cut in the benefits it pays to employees generally, including Jennifer, and wanted to keep that information from employees until it made a decision. Or suppose Jennifer were considering a career change. The benefits information would be important in Jennifer's decision and Jennifer's possible career change would be important information for Fanatical. The problem is that when you represent two clients on a single matter, their communications are not privileged from one another. Put differently, a lawyer cannot refuse to disclose to one of a pair of joint clients information that the other client has given to the lawyer when that information is material to the representation of the first client. This means that a lawyer representing both Jennifer and the entity would have to be very careful to avoid acquiring such information in the first place. And, of course, these sorts of possibilities should be explicitly spelled out in the information given both clients in obtaining their informed consent to the conflict.

your part. If, for example, anyone on the Board seems like she will launch into a discussion of Jennifer's performance as CEO, you remind her that you do not represent Fanatical as to Jennifer's employment issues and that you must excuse yourself from the discussion so as not to compromise your position as lawyer either for Jennifer or the Board.

Jennifer has now approached you with a prospective deal that she would like your professional assistance with. She owns a small estate just outside of town that would be ideal as a satellite office for Fanatical. She has had preliminary discussions with Board members and Fanatical may be interested in buying it. Both Fanatical and Jennifer would like you to represent them in connection with the sale.

Task Two:

Write down the ways that these client interests may come into conflict in the process of negotiating and completing this real estate sale. After you have written your answer, consult Self-Assessment 2 for Exercise L on the LexisNexis web course.

Task Three:

Reviewing what you have learned about inter-client conflicts of interest and the limitations on a lawyer's representation of clients with conflicting interests, do you think you can represent both clients in this transaction? Do you have enough facts to have an opinion? Consider these Official Comments to Model Rule 1.7:

> [7] Directly adverse conflicts can also arise in transactional matters. For example, if a lawyer is asked to represent the seller of a business in negotiations with a buyer represented by the lawyer, not in the same transaction but in another, unrelated matter, the lawyer could not undertake the representation without the informed consent of each client.

> [28] Whether a conflict is consentable depends on the circumstances. For example, a lawyer may not represent multiple parties to a negotiation whose interests are fundamentally antagonistic to each other, but common representation is permissible where the clients are generally aligned in interest even though there is some difference in interest among them.

Write down your answer and explanation, your qualified answer and explanation, or the kinds of facts you will need in order to make an intelligent answer. After you have written your answer, consult Self-Assessment 3 for Exercise L on the LexisNexis web course.

Task Four:

Jennifer and Fanatical have clarified that they are going to hammer out the terms of the deal and, once those terms are set, simply want you to prepare the sales contract for both of them to sign. On the basis of that, you "reasonably believe" that you "will be able to provide competent and diligent representation to each affected client." The rules require that you still need to get the informed consent as defined above of both to this representation.

You will have to get informed consent from each of them to the conflict of interest that this situation presents. That informed consent should address the advantages and disadvantages of joint representation and the problems that might develop with a joint representation.

Please make a list of the points that should be covered in the document that will solicit the two clients' informed consent to your joint representation. Remember that you want to be certain that the clients have enough information to consent to the dual representation. We have asked a well-respected practicing lawyer to create a version of consent for this setting. You can see what he thought important and how he articulated the points in Self-Assessment 4 for Exercise L on the LexisNexis web course.

Chapter 13

HELPING A CLIENT COPE WITH INSECURITY ABOUT CONTRACT PERFORMANCE

PREVIEW

In this Chapter we again will focus on how lawyers participate in the resolution of contract performance problems (at least two other chapters focus on this kind of contract work). In this variation, there is a long-term contract where the client's contracting partner has become late in its payment obligations and may be showing signs of financial distress.

Often, clients work through their contract performance problems by negotiating, threatening, or cajoling without the help of lawyers. Indeed, there is far more give-and-take in the performance of complicated contracts than we see in most first-year Contract materials, focused as they are on contracts that have collapsed. But clients and their lawyers, when they get involved, typically engage in a great many remediation attempts before they throw in the towel and go to litigation. Sometimes the performance problem is solved through a contract modification. For example, if the person supplying the goods or performing the service has encountered performance difficulties — let's say, its own costs have gone up — its contracting partner may well grant a concession and renegotiate the price upwards. Getting the work done or the goods supplied is often more important to the person receiving the goods and services than is insisting on a good deal originally negotiated.

In real life, a contract performance problem might not come to a lawyer until the client had exhausted other options. Moving forward without a lawyer is probably a good idea if the client thereby solves most of the problems herself; it becomes a bad thing if, in the process of attempting to solve its problem, the client made matters worse. Part of a business lawyer's work involves educating clients to work through their own problems in a way that is not harmful to their legal position, should their efforts fail.

As with most materials designed for law students, we simplify the facts and make them slightly artificial for pedagogical reasons.

SUBSTANTIVE CONTENT:

- UCC § 2-306 requirements and output contracts
- UCC § 2-609 and demands for assurance
- UCC § 2-208 course of performance in contract interpretation
- UCC § 2-612 installment contracts

SKILLS AND VALUES UTILIZED:

- Advising a client about how to respond to repeated breaches in an ongoing contract.
- Preventing inadvertent modification (through course of performance) of an ongoing contract.
- Drafting and using contract terms to avoid predictable problems and reduce uncertainty.

ESTIMATED TIME FOR COMPLETION: 60 Minutes

LEVEL OF DIFFICULTY (1 to 3):

EXERCISE M:

Memo

To: YOU

From: Harry Harumph, Esq.

Re: Gratsci's Grease Contract Problem

Our client, Gratsci's Grease, supplies grease to automobile repair shops all over the East Coast. Typically, it makes "requirements contracts" with the shops where it agrees to supply the shop's "requirements"[1] for grease at a fixed price per quart, over the course of the year. The form sales contract calls for each buyer to pay for the preceding month's delivery in cash or cash equivalent within 30 days of the last delivery.

The problem is that the buyer, Conichetti Chrysler, has been running late in its payments. Two months ago, it paid its bill 35 days after delivery and this past month it paid 40 days after delivery. What's worse, Conichetti isn't the only one. Several of the other car dealer / repair shops that Gratsci's supplies are doing

---

[1] The UCC explicitly permits parties to contract for the supply of a buyer's "requirements" or for the buyer to buy all of the seller's "output." The quantity sold in these contracts is, obviously, not a fixed amount but the amount that the buyer needs or the seller produces as long as the output or requirements are stated in good faith. While these contracts were called too "indefinite" for enforcement by earlier courts, they are now widely used and not controversial. *See* UCC § 2-306.

the same thing. The client made a big stink after Conicetti's first late payment in an effort to get the payments back on track but, obviously, was unsuccessful. Gratsci's wants to see if we can be more successful in getting Conichetti to pay on time going forward and, if we are successful with them, use that approach on other buyers. Our services will pay for themselves if we can successfully help Gratsci's improve its general experience with its accounts receivable.

The client also perceived a larger problem: that repeatedly accepting late payments might inadvertently modify the contract. I even remember from *my* contracts class that late payments are usually (depending on how the contract is read) breaches of contract. The problems are 1) that a late payment can be perceived as trivial (and therefore not grounds for canceling the contract) and 2) that a series of late payments could effectively create a modification of the contract if the seller acquiesces in them.[2]

I'm sure you remember better than I do, from the jumble of legal principles gathered under the heading "conditions" and "performance," that a seller may not be entitled to cancel an installment contract solely because of the buyer's single late payment. While this is a very murky and difficult area, suffice it to say that the common law and the applicable sections of the Uniform Commercial Code tend towards the conclusion that a late payment by a buyer in an installment contract does not permit the seller to retaliate by terminating the entire contract; it may not even be enough to allow the seller to suspend its own performance. I flipped through the Uniform Commercial Code and found a section on installment contracts[3] that, basically, requires the equivalent of a "material breach" before a client can suspend its own performance. I have learned from a little hornbook research that the client's suspending its performance in the absence of a "material breach" could expose our own client to liability for breach of contract and that suspension may become a "material breach." We certainly do not what to expose our client to liability.

---

[2] The UCC makes this explicit. UCC § 2-208 provides:

   (1) Where the contract for sale involves repeated occasions for performance by either party with knowledge of the nature of the performance and opportunity for objection to it by the other, any course of performance accepted or acquiesced in without objection shall be relevant to determine the meaning of the agreement.

Revised Article 1 of the UCC now defines a course of performance in 1-303 as:

   (a) A "course of performance" is a sequence of conduct between the parties to a particular transaction that exists if:

      (1) the agreement of the parties with respect to the transaction involves repeated occasions for performance by a party; and

      (2) the other party, with knowledge of the nature of the performance and opportunity for objection to it, accepts the performance or acquiesces in it without objection.

[3] UCC § 2-612.

Task One:

The client has asked us what to do when Gratsci's is given a late payment. Rejecting the payment is, from the client's perspective, out of the question — the client's father, who founded the company, always said "*never* turn down a payment." But the client wants to make sure that accepting a late payment is not later seen as a modification of the payment date.

Please prepare for my review a customizable form letter for the client to send its buyers when their payments are late so that accepting the late payments will not later be interpreted as acquiescing to a later payment schedule than what is in the original contract. After you have written your answer, consult Self-Assessment 1 for Exercise M on the LexisNexis web course.

Task Two:

In the process of addressing this problem, the client asked that we look at the underlying form sales contract that was drafted by a predecessor lawyer a couple of years ago. I have found nothing in the contract addressing the question of late payments. Please draft a paragraph to include in the sales contract that will reduce the odds in *future* contracts that the client's accepting late payments will be seen as acquiescence to a change in the payment schedule originally specified in the contract. Use plain, clear English — always better than legalese. After you have written your answer, consult Self-Assessment 2 for Exercise M on the LexisNexis web course.

With the payment period slipping, your client is beginning to get worried (particularly with respect to the several Chrysler dealerships it supplies) that it is going to be left unpaid for some portion of its delivered grease. Uniform Commercial Code § 2-609 was designed to address situations like this. It provides in relevant part:

§ 2-609. Right to Adequate Assurance of Performance

(1) A contract for sale imposes an obligation on each party that the other's expectation of receiving due performance will not be impaired. When reasonable grounds for insecurity arise with respect to the performance of either party the other may in writing demand adequate assurance of due performance and until he receives such assurance may, if commercially reasonable, suspend any performance for which he has not already received the agreed return.

.

.

.

(4) After receipt of a justified demand failure to provide within a reasonable time not exceeding thirty days such assurance of

due performance as is adequate under the circumstances of the particular case is a repudiation of the contract.

A translation might help. In response to "reasonable grounds for insecurity," subsection 1 of this provision effectively permits the aggrieved party to unilaterally modify the contract by demanding an "assurance" and impose that modified contract onto the other side. Failure to provide this assurance is a "repudiation" under subsection 4 and that repudiation will permit the initially aggrieved party to terminate the contract without liability for doing so. Since the non-breaching party is responding with a unilateral modification of the contract, you can expect this power will be very limited and that it might be risky to use it.

The statute requires that the user have "reasonable grounds for insecurity" in order to use the provision. That requires a very nuanced judgment in many cases; the statute does not protect a demand for assurance without reasonable grounds for making it. In such a case, the maker of the demand would simply be demanding more than is permissible under the contract and could, by doing so, breach the contract itself. In addition, there is, obviously, a proportionality built into the statute: even with "reasonable grounds for insecurity," you cannot demand an assurance that is more than "adequate under the circumstances" and then terminate for repudiation. That action will convert your own termination into a breach.

Task Three:

By a strange coincidence, Mr. Harumph has encountered 2-609 in his further excursions into the UCC. He has recognized that Gratsci's has not supplied you with very rich facts, but wants your thoughts on whether your client has "reasonable grounds for insecurity" in the Conicetti case. His follow-up is that "if you think there are reasonable grounds, what "assurance" would/could Gratsci's demand? Spend a few minutes thinking it through and then come to discuss this."

Please put your answer in the form of talking points or notes for the discussion you will have with Mr. Harumph.[4] After you have written your answer, consult Self-Assessment 3 for Exercise M on the LexisNexis web course.

If you have understood this problem so far, you have a sense of how devilishly hard it is use § 2-609 in the field: indeed, if you were able to give Harumph a clear, straight answer to his § 2-609 question, you probably did not appreciate the difficulties of the § 2-609

---

[4] HINT: Asking Conicetti's to "assure us that your payments will be on time in the future" could be a non-starter. There is no downside for Conicetti's to respond by making such an assurance and then being late again. Since only a failure to give assurance leads to a repudiation, if the recipient gives the assurance that you have demanded, the breacher has complied with the statute. In that case, you'll probably have to start over.

process. You have to guess what a court will later see as 1) "reasonable grounds for insecurity" and 2) then construct a meaningful demand that you can predict a later court will see as "reasonable" under the circumstances.

When a client can anticipate performance problems in a contractual relationship, it is usually worth thinking about whether they can be solved, or at least made more manageable, in the contract itself. We worked on a form of that earlier, in Task Two, when we drafted a contract provision intended to preserve the payment schedule in the contract.

You have no doubt seen contract clauses in contracts providing that "time is of the essence" or that a late payment is a "material breach." These are, obviously, attempts to make what might be perceived as a trivial breach into something more "material," thereby giving the payee a better justification for terminating the contract on account of the late payment. But these provisions are not foolproof either: repeatedly *not* making good on such a provision might be found to be a waiver of the provision, whatever the provision might say.[5] And given that a seller wants to continue selling - its buyers are really its *customers* — a seller's natural tendency might be to accept the late payments instead of terminating. Let's try something different.

Task Four:

Harumph, intrigued by § 2-609 but annoyed at its vagary, wants you to create language to put into Gratsci's form sales contract that will reduce the uncertainty inherent in using the provision. He has asked you to construct no more than 3 paragraphs for the contract that will permit Gratsci's to use § 2-609 with less uncertainty than you would have without a contract provision. You will want to define what is "reasonable grounds" and you will want to state some "assurance" that you will define as appropriate under the circumstances. After you have written your answer, consult Self-Assessment 4 on the LexisNexis web course.

---

[5] None other than the Supreme Court of the United States so held in the 19th Century in a life insurance case, *Ins. Co. v. Norton*, 96 U.S. 234 (1878). In *Norton*, the insurance policy stated that a late payment would yield a forfeiture of the policy benefits, yet the company routinely accepted late payments. When the insured died and the company promptly denied coverage, the question was whether the company had effectively waived the forfeiture provision. The Court sustained a jury finding that the provision was waived by the company's conduct. Hundreds of courts have made similar decisions since then in many different contexts.

Chapter 14
ANALYZING AND INTERPRETING A PRENUPTIAL AGREEMENT

PREVIEW

Practicing family law requires knowledge of many areas of the law such as tax law, substantive family law, and contracts. In this Chapter we introduce you to one intersection of contract law and family law: the prenuptial agreement. Although other areas of the law will impact prenuptial agreements, this chapter focuses on their contracting aspects.

In this Chapter, you will read and attempt to interpret a reasonably-standard prenuptial agreement. The wife is seriously ill with Alzheimer's Disease and the husband is healthy. Depending on how one interprets the prenuptial agreement, payment for her care will come either from her healthy husband or from her estate that is controlled by her adult daughter from an earlier marriage who serves as her attorney in fact. While this Chapter is largely about contract interpretation, in the process you will necessarily learn a little about family law and about the role that contract law plays within this area of legal practice.

SUBSTANTIVE CONTENT:

- Premarital Agreements — Uniform Premarital Agreement Act
- Restatement (2d) Contracts § 190
- Interpretation in contracts
- The Parol Evidence Rule

SKILLS AND VALUES UTILIZED:

- Reading a premarital contract to determine what portions of the agreement may help a client's arguments, what clauses may support an opposite argument, and what clauses are not relevant.

- Developing legal arguments based on a file when the client is unavailable or unable to help.

- Assessing a case: determining what additional facts you need from a client to help answer the question asked by the client.

- Use of a merger clause and how it might fit into a dispute such as this.

- Statutory interpretation.

ESTIMATED TIME FOR COMPLETION: 90 Minutes

LEVEL OF DIFFICULTY (1 to 5):

Contracts, Family Law, and Prenuptial Agreements:

Contracts, as you know, are used in a wide array of circumstances, including situations we would ordinarily think of as "family law." A common example is a contract between two people who wish to determine before marriage how to divide their individual and joint property, deal with debts, spousal support, and a variety of other issues in the event of death, annulment, or divorce. These types of contracts are called ante-nuptial or prenuptial, or premarital agreements; we will refer to them here as "prenuptial agreements." They were not enforced widely until the mid 1970s because of public policy concerns that enforcing them would encourage divorce and harm children. Since the late 1970s, however, courts have become much more amenable to enforcing these types of agreements.

Although prenuptial contracts are notorious among celebrities,[1] they are becoming more widely used today by more ordinary people. In addition to resolving financial matters in the event of death or divorce, an attorney may draft a prenuptial agreement to incorporate various responsibilities for each spouse during the marriage including everything from who is responsible for household chores to keeping the family checkbook. While these may be useful to a couple in planning and dividing household work, many such non-economic provisions would not be enforceable — how would a court place a value on "taking out the dog" or "preparing healthy dinners" or evaluate

---

[1] An interesting celebrity prenuptial agreement is the one between Catherine Zeta-Jones and Michael Douglas. They included in their agreement a clause that provided, if they divorced, Zeta-Jones would receive $2.8 million for every year they had been married. Plus, if she could prove Douglas cheated on her, she would be entitled to a one-time payment of $5 million. A few other unusual clauses reported by divorce lawyers, although of dubious enforceability, are a requirement of random drug tests with a penalty if the spouse failed the test; a right to the other spouse's frequent flier miles in the event of adultery; and a requirement that a husband may only watch one football game on Sundays during the football season. *See* Split Ends, Chicago Sun Times by Jae-Ha-Kim, September 29, 2004.

the performance of such tasks if the breaching party were ordered to do them?[2]

Although non-economic commitments may have some difficulty being enforced through contract law, premarital agreements that attempt to spell out the financial aspects of the relationship have had more luck. The Restatement (Second) of Contracts and the Uniform Premarital Agreement Act[3] have now recognized the importance of prenuptial contracts and allow for enforceability unless an agreement violates public policy.

Prenuptial agreements are ordinary contracts, subject to the usual contract rules, but with a substantial public policy overlay. Generally, as long as both parties entered into the agreement voluntarily and both parties fully disclosed their property interests, they are enforceable contracts. But, given the involvement of the state in family law matters, we can expect regulation by statute and in the courts on grounds of public policy. For example, one might expect a public policy exception to thwart an attempt by one parent to bargain away his or her obligation to support a child.[4]

Interpretation issues are quite common in prenuptial agreements. Imagine the clause mentioned in footnote 1 that limits a husband to watching only one football game on Sundays during the football season. Although that term likely would not be enforceable, we can use it to illustrate how an apparently straightforward term may in fact be subject to more than one interpretation. Can you think of interpretation problems that may occur with that type of clause? A few that come to mind are whether this means only professional football typically played on Sundays or would it also include college games that are sometimes (but not usually) played on Sundays? Can the husband watch two games in one "game interval" through picture-in-picture or similar technology? Does the provision extend into the post-season period to include playoff games or just the regular season?

EXERCISE N:[5]

One of the senior attorneys in your firm, Michael Partner, recently gave you several files that he wants you to review involving prenuptial

---

[2] An example of the types of clauses that a court probably would not enforce can be illustrated by a prenuptial agreement that a couple Rex and Teresa LeGalley, reportedly signed in Albuquerque, New Mexico in 1995. Their 16-page agreement covered everything from financial matters, the type of gas to use in their cars, how to shop for groceries, and when belongings must be picked up from the bedroom floor. Those types of non-economic clauses likely are not enforceable and not the type of agreement that one would expect to see litigated in court. *See Morrow v. Morrow*, 612 P. 2d 730, 732 (Okla. App. 1980) (noting the general principle that family arrangements are presumed not to have contractual consequences, although it is a rebuttable presumption).

[3] The Uniform Premarital Agreement Act was drafted by the National Conference of Commissioners on Uniform State Laws in 1983 and has been enacted in over 25 states.

[4] *See* The Uniform Premarital Agreement Act, Section (3) (a), (b) stating that parents may not enter an agreement that adversely affects the right to child support.

[5] This problem is loosely based on the case of *Homra v. Nelson*, 2008 Tenn. App. Lexis 148.

agreements. Michael told you that, although he knows there may be specific family law issues, tax issues, and other issues involved with prenuptial agreements, he is not concerned with those at this time. Instead, he wants you to review the documents in the files solely for contract issues. He has other Associates in the firm evaluating the case from the other angles.

The first file contains a prenuptial agreement between Tony and Molly Slade. Before heading off to court, Michael told you that Sandy Fair, the daughter of Mrs. Slade, had retained the firm to determine who is responsible for the medical care of her mother who was recently diagnosed with Alzheimer's disease – is it her mother or her stepfather? Mr. Partner wants your view as to whether the prenuptial agreement will answer Ms. Fair's questions or if you think the issues are so complicated that it may require protracted litigation, something that Ms. Fair obviously wants to avoid. As you will learn below, since much of Mrs. Slade's property will pass to Ms. Fair on Mrs. Slade's death, Ms. Fair has an obvious financial interest in the resolution of this matter.

Your review of the file and interview with Ms. Fair revealed the following information: Ms. Fair's mother, Molly Fair, married Tony Slade ten years ago when they were both 68 years of age and in good health. Because of their age, the fact that they each had adult children from a previous marriage, and that this was the second marriage for both of them, they agreed to sign a prenuptial contract so they could specify some of the financial responsibilities for each of them during the marriage as well as what would happen in the event of divorce, annulment, or death.[6] Both Tony and Molly have significant wealth, most of it in property holdings; however, Mr. Slade is much wealthier than his wife. The Slades had attorneys who represented each of them[7] when the prenuptial agreement was drafted and signed, although Mrs. Slade's previous attorney has since retired, moved out of town, and is no longer practicing law.[8]

The Slades lived a very happy life until last year when Mrs. Slade's health took a turn for the worse. Molly Slade became increasingly forgetful and had a difficult time doing the sort of everyday chores that many of us take for granted such as walking the dog, doing the grocery

---

[6] This common kind of agreement is often made to preserve each spouse's assets for their own children, should anything be left when they die.

[7] It should be common practice to have a lawyer represent each of the parties to a prenuptial agreement. The potential for overreaching by either party in the negotiations in the prenuptial setting means that such agreements concluded without such representation are *very* fragile and will likely encounter difficulties in enforcement.

[8] **Sidebar** provided by Barbara Atwood, the Mary Ann Richey Professor of Law, at the University of Arizona Rogers College of Law in Tucson, Arizona.

Although the ideal may be that independent counsel represents each party to a premarital agreement, this is not always the reality and it is a significant issue in enforcement of premarital agreements. Some states impose a presumption of lack of voluntariness if counsel does not represent each party. For example, Cal. Fam. Code § 1615 (West 2002) provides that a premarital agreement is not voluntary unless a court determines that the party contesting enforcement was either represented by independent legal counsel when the agreement was signed or signs a written waiver after being advised to seek independent legal counsel.

shopping, getting to doctor's appointments, returning telephone calls, and other routine matters. Eventually, Mrs. Slade began to have such serious memory problems that she had trouble functioning in her home without someone to help her. Additionally, Tony began to have a number of health problems, so he was not able to care for Molly.

When Molly's health and memory problems began, she signed a durable power of attorney that gave her daughter, Sandy Fair, permission to act as Molly's attorney in fact[9] should she be unable to do so. Shortly after that, upon the recommendation of the family doctor, Molly Slade went to live in an assisted living facility. Because Tony had some health problems and he desired to continue living with his wife, he moved into the assisted living apartment with Molly. Begrudgingly, Sandy liquidated some of her mother's assets to help pay for the assisted living apartment and Tony paid his monthly living expenses from his own assets, though Sandy maintained all along that Tony Slade should have paid for his wife's living expenses at the apartment. Until the memory problems started, Molly was quite healthy and there is nothing in her medical history or the family medical history that would have indicated that she might be diagnosed with Alzheimer's disease or any other illness that would require long-term health care.

Shortly after Molly went to live in the assisted living apartment, she was diagnosed with Alzheimer's disease. That disease eventually causes the deterioration of an individual's memory and other abilities to the point that the person with Alzheimer's loses the capacity to function on her own, even with the help of an assisted living facility. As a result of the progressing Alzheimer's disease, Molly needed to be placed in a secure facility for Alzheimer's patients that was in a different building from the assisted living apartment that the couple shared. The Alzheimer's home is state of the art, with a reputation for providing the highest quality of care for Alzheimer's patients. It caters to a fairly wealthy clientele, is difficult to get into, and does not accept any Medicaid payments. Since the Slade's did not purchase long-term health care insurance, the payment for Molly's care would have to come entirely from the Slade's funds or insurance. There were no viable alternatives to this care facility—others either had long waiting lists or were clearly inferior.

After Molly's diagnosis, Mr. Slade signed a document rescinding the agreement for his wife to be in the assisted living apartment, so she could be transferred to the Alzheimer's home. The following week, he sent Ms. Fair a copy of the rescinded agreement and a notice that she needed to begin to pay for her mother's expenses in the Alzheimer's home out of her mother's finances because he was invoking the premarital contract.

---

[9] A "power of attorney" authorizes and appoints an "attorney in fact" to act on that person's behalf in legal, medical, or business matters. The document itself, typically notarized, is often called the power of attorney. The "attorney in fact" can be anyone and clearly need not be an attorney at law (lawyer). While they share the word "attorney" the two are completely different. There is a substantial body of law defining the obligations of a person appointed through a power of attorney.

In other words, he declared that he was not responsible for his wife's care. Sandy tried to reason with her stepfather and insisted that it was his responsibility to pay for her mother's care in the Alzheimer's facility but the two of them reached an impasse on this issue.

Tony told Sandy that, before signing the premarital agreement, he and his wife had talked about the possibility that one of them would need long-term care. During that conversation they each had agreed to bear responsibility for their own care, so as not to burden the other spouse. Like most people, they believed at the time that neither of them would need long-term care. According to Tony, since both of the Slades were healthy and did not foresee any illnesses that might require long-term care, they did not bother to put this agreement in the prenuptial contract and they never told either of their attorneys.

Sandy has asked the firm to help her determine whether she must liquidate some of her mother's assets to pay for the Alzheimer's facility. She believes that it is her stepfather's responsibility to care for her mother and that she should not have to use her mother's assets to pay for her care. Sandy told you that the Alzheimer's facility where her mother is living is quite expensive. Molly's assets likely only will cover her care for four or five years before her money runs out and she could live much longer than that. Sandy knows that Tony Slade has considerable property holdings throughout the state and she believes he could easily pay for her mother's care without it making a significant dent in his assets. Sandy suspects he does not want to spend the money because he wants to leave all of it to his children from a previous marriage.

Task One:

The file contains a copy of the prenuptial agreement, which contains 14 paragraphs (we have deleted the first to avoid confusion). The agreement sorts out the responsibilities of each spouse by reference to the assets each had before the marriage and to certain financial responsibilities during the marriage. Exhibits "A" and "B" (omitted from the problem) were attached to the agreement and they were an accurate summary of each party's assets and liabilities. Read the prenuptial agreement between Tony and Molly Slade and 1) highlight the paragraph or paragraphs of the agreement that you believe will be relevant to answering Sandy's questions about who will bear the financial responsibility for her mother's care in the Alzheimer's facility and 2) state *why* you believe the paragraph will be relevant. After you have selected the paragraphs that may be important to answering the client's question, 3) prioritize them in the order (from best to worst) in which they will help Ms. Fair's ability to secure payment from Mr. Slade for her mother's care. The priority order should be from most helpful to most hurtful of her case. You might find a spreadsheet such as Excel to be a convenient way to organize, sort, and memorialize your impressions.

After completing this task, consult Self-Assessment 1 for Exercise N on the LexisNexis web course.

STATE OF BLISS   )

)

)

)

COUNTY OF DOLLARS   )

PRENUPTIAL AGREEMENT BETWEEN TONY SLADE AND MOLLY FAIR[10]

This agreement is entered into between Tony Slade, herein referred to as Tony, and Molly Fair, herein referred to as Molly.

The parties to this agreement are not at this time married to each other nor to any other person, and they contemplate becoming married to each other in the near future. This agreement is entered into for the purpose of determining the rights, duties and obligations between themselves and unto each other in the event they are subsequently married and if such marriage is thereafter terminated by annulment, divorce, or death. Both parties agree that entering into this agreement is good and valuable consideration, including the consideration herein expressed, and the love and consideration they have for one another, including the entry of the parties into marriage to each other, the sufficiency of all considerations are hereby acknowledged; they both agree not to challenge this agreement for lack of consideration or any other reason; and acknowledge and agree that they will hereafter be estopped from making any challenge to this agreement.

Therefore, for the considerations herein expressed, the parties warrant and represent unto each other and agree as follows:

1. Intent of Agreement. [omitted material about rights in the absence of agreement]

2. Statements of Financial Worth. Exhibit, "A" which is attached hereto, represents a general statement of the current financial net worth of Tony Slade. Exhibit "B" which is attached hereto represents a general statement of the current financial net worth of Molly Fair.

3. Assets at the Time of Marriage. In the event of marriage, both parties will keep and maintain their current assets in their individual names and ownership, together with any contribution or addition thereto during marriage, and growth and appreciation thereon during marriage, including proceeds, dividends, interest, proceeds of liquidation of any asset, and reinvestment of any such proceeds, growth,

---

[10] Thanks to Judge Billy Bell, family court judge in Huntsville, Alabama, for permitting us to adapt an agreement he drafted while in practice for use in this chapter.

dividends or interest. In the event of the termination of the marriage by annulment or divorce, or the death of Tony Slade during the marriage, Molly Fair shall receive nothing from his separate estate, and expressly waives all claims of spousal rights and all other rights that she otherwise may lawfully have to receive any other benefit by virtue of their marriage or his death; and Molly agrees not to assert or make any such claim, and acknowledges that she is forever estopped in that regard. In the event of the termination of the marriage by annulment or divorce, or the death of Molly Fair during the marriage, Tony Slade shall receive nothing from her separate estate, and expressly waives all claims of spousal rights and all other rights that he otherwise may lawfully have to receive any other benefit by virtue of their marriage or her death; and Tony agrees not to assert or make any such claim, and acknowledges that he is forever estopped in that regard.

4. <u>Payment of Daily Living Expenses.</u> During the marriage, Mr. Slade shall be responsible for providing food and other daily necessities for the parties following their marriage.

5. <u>Last Will and Testament and Jointly Owned Property.</u> The parties are not precluded from making the other party a beneficiary under a Last Will and Testament, this being a matter that is left in the sole discretion of each party. Should either party be specifically named as a beneficiary under the Last Will and Testament of the other party, then and in that event the beneficiary shall receive the benefits bestowed under the Last Will and Testament of the other party, in addition to any rights and benefits herein provided. Any household furniture, goods and belongings, including appliances, which are acquired by the parties during the marriage, shall be conclusively presumed to be owned by them jointly. In the event the anticipated marriage is terminated by annulment or divorce, each party is to receive one half (1/2) of such household furniture, goods, and belongings."

6. <u>Marital Estate and Arbitration.</u> Any joint business venture, joint checking account, joint savings account, joint security account, joint investment or real property acquired in their joint names shall be deemed to be the joint property of the parties and constitute the marital estate. In the event of Tony's death during marriage, Molly shall receive the entirety of such marital estate (as such term is heretofore defined). In the event of Molly's death during marriage, Tony shall

---

[11] **Sidebar: "Joint property"**

    Property that is "jointly held" becomes the sole property of the surviving person when the other dies. This is an implication of a "joint tenancy" about which you will learn in the Property course.

receive the entirety of such marital estate (as such term is heretofore defined). In the event the anticipated marriage is dissolved by annulment or divorce, for purposes of this agreement, fifty percent (50%) of such marital estate is conclusively presumed to belong to Tony and fifty percent (50%) thereof conclusively presumed to belong to Molly, and the same shall be distributed accordingly. If the parties cannot agree on such distribution, they each agree to appoint a representative to make an appraisal, an evaluation, and a suggested plan of distribution; in the event they do not agree, those two designated representatives are authorized to select a third person, and the three designated people will make an appraisal, an evaluation, and a suggested plan of distribution by majority vote which will be binding upon the parties to this agreement. Both parties agree to accept and be bound by such process. It is agreed that the majority decision of the arbitrators shall be binding upon the parties. Both parties agree to execute all documents and papers necessary, requisite or proper to effectuate such arbitration process and plan of distribution of the marital estate.

7. <u>Medical Needs and Treatment</u>. Both Tony and Molly receive Medicare at the present time and they each carry a Medicare Supplement, which provides for any medical expenses, which Medicare does not cover. Each party shall continue to pay his or her Medicare and Medicare Supplement policy expenses on a timely basis and from his or her separate property. Each party shall carry that amount of medical insurance, to include hospitalization, to provide for his or her foreseeable medical requirements. The charges for all such medical insurance shall be paid for by that person who is to receive the medical benefits from the policies. He or she shall pay for such medical protection from his or her separate property.

8. <u>Current liabilities.</u> Both parties acknowledge that neither is the subject of pending lawsuits or have any known contingent liabilities.

9. <u>Liability for Debts</u>. Each party shall be solely responsible for paying for all debts incurred prior to their wedding. The property of the other party to this agreement shall not be liable to seizure or execution for such debts. In the same manner, all debts after marriage unless clearly stated to be the responsibility of the other party, or a mutual responsibility, shall be the sole obligation of the party incurring the debt.

10. <u>Filing for divorce or annulment.</u> In the event of the filing of an action by either party for the termination of the anticipated marriage by annulment or divorce, neither party shall

make any claim for alimony, or for payment of attorney's fees incurred; and in the event of annulment or divorce, they waive any such claims against the other, and in the separate estate of the other, except as may herein be specifically provided.

11. Execution of Necessary Documents. Both parties agree to execute and deliver any other instruments or documents necessary to give effect to the provisions of this agreement.

12. Modifications or Rescission of Agreement. This agreement may be modified, amended, or rescinded at any time after the solemnization of the marriage between the parties only by a subsequent written agreement signed by both parties.

13. Inspection of Accounts. Each party acknowledges that prior to the execution of this agreement that they have been given full opportunity, both personally and through their attorney, their accountant, or such other representative as they may wish to designate, to make a full and complete inspection of all books, documents, records and tax returns of the other party and they are fully and fairly advised of the net worth of the other party.

14. Integration. Tony and Molly agree that this document contains the full and complete agreement between the parties and that there are no other agreements, understandings, conditions, or promises outside of this agreement.

IN WITNESS WHEREOF, the parties have executed this agreement on this 31st day of August, year 0000.

/S/   *Tony Slade*
_____
Tony Slade

/S/   *Molly Fair*
_____
Molly Fair

STATE OF BLISS)

)

)

)

COUNTY OF DOLLARS)

I, the undersigned, a Notary Public in and for said County and State, hereby certify that Tony Slade, whose name is signed to the foregoing Premarital Agreement, and who is known to me, acknowledged before me on this day that, being informed of the contents of said Premarital Agreement, he executed the same voluntarily on this date.

GIVEN under my hand and official seal this the 31st day of August, 0000.

Nancy M. Notary
_____

/S/   *Nancy M. Notary*
_____
NOTARY PUBLIC

September 1, 0000
My Commission Expires: _____

STATE OF BLISS)

)

)

)

COUNTY OF DOLLARS)

I, the undersigned, a Notary Public in and for said County and State, hereby certify that Molly Fair, whose name is signed to the foregoing Premarital Agreement, and who is known to me, acknowledged before me on this day that, being informed of the contents of said Premarital Agreement, he executed the same voluntarily on this date.

GIVEN under my hand and official seal this the 31st day of August, 0000.

Nancy M. Notary
_____

/S/   *Nancy M. Notary*
_____
NOTARY PUBLIC

September 1, 0000
My Commission Expires: _____

Task Two:

Make a bullet list of any important evidence *not in the Prenuptial Agreement* that you have gathered from the file or your interview with Sandy Fair that may impact the questions raised by Sandy Fair and state why they may be important.

After you have written your answer, consult Self-Assessment 2 for Exercise N on the LexisNexis web course.

Task Three:

You realize that you should see if the law of your state would enforce premarital agreements. Your research found that the State of Bliss has enacted the Uniform Premarital Agreement Act. First, review the Act and pertinent sections of the Restatement (Second) of Contracts printed below and make some notes about whether you think the law will present an obstacle to enforcing the premarital agreement and why.

After you have written your answer, consult Self-Assessment 3 for Exercise N on the LexisNexis web course.

The Uniform Premarital Agreement Act

Section 3

    a) Parties to a premarital agreement may contract with respect to:

    (1) the rights and obligations of each of the parties in any of the property of either or both of them whenever and wherever acquired or located;

    (2) the right to buy, sell, use, transfer, exchange, abandon, lease, consume, expend, assign, create a security interest in, mortgage, encumber, dispose of, or otherwise manage and control property;

    (3) the disposition of property upon separation, marital dissolution, death, or the occurrence or nonoccurrence of any other event;

    (4) the modification or elimination of spousal support;

    (5) the making of a will, trust, or other arrangement to carry out the provisions of the agreement;

    (6) the ownership rights in and disposition of the death benefit from a life insurance policy;

    (7) the choice of law governing the construction of the agreement; and

(8) any other matter, including their personal rights and obligations, not in violation of public policy or a statute imposing
a criminal penalty.

(b) The right of a child to support may not be adversely affected
by a premarital agreement.

Restatement (2d) of Contracts Section 190:

(1) A promise by a person contemplating marriage or by a
married person, other than as part of an enforceable separation agreement, is unenforceable on grounds of public
policy if it would change some essential incident of the
marital relationship in a way detrimental to the public
interest in the marriage relationship. A separation agreement is unenforceable on grounds of public policy unless it
is made after separation or in contemplation of an immediate separation and is fair in the circumstances.

(2) A promise that tends unreasonably to encourage divorce or
separation is unenforceable on grounds of public policy.

Task Four:

Read again paragraphs 4, 7, and 9 in the prenuptial agreement that
are pertinent to the questions asked by Sandy. How would a lawyer use
those provisions in an argument about who must pay for Ms. Slade's
care? Summarize the arguments for each side using the document's
paragraphs to support the argument as needed. After you have written
your answer, consult Self-Assessment 4 for Exercise N on the LexisNexis
web course.

Task Five:

Think about what interpretive issues from contract law you will
need to research before making a demand letter to Mr. Slade on
Sandy's behalf and particularly those that stem from the merger
clause appearing in Paragraph 14. If you have not studied the Parol
Evidence Rule or need a refresher, go to the Web to access the Parole
Evidence Rule refresher. Write a list of the major issues and sub
issues from the concepts in the refresher. As you do this, make note
of any specific words in the agreement that you think may be particularly important and why.

After you have written your answer, consult Self-Assessment 5 for
Exercise N on the LexisNexis web course.

Chapter 15

DRAFTING A PUBLIC HOUSING EVICTION COMPLAINT BASED ON BREACH OF A LEASE

PREVIEW

In property law you probably will encounter (or have encountered) the residential lease. The landlord-tenant relationship has evolved over time and is ingrained in both contract and property law. You may recall from your own experience that it is not uncommon for a landlord to require a tenant to sign a lease delineating each other's rights and responsibilities. Most jurisdictions, if not all, have local ordinances and state statutes that define many of the legal responsibilities between the landlord and tenant.[1] These may include such things as a requirement that a residence be habitable, specific steps that must occur before an eviction may occur, what a landlord may do with a deposit from a tenant, and other quite specific guidelines that regulate the relationship between landlords and tenants in residential leases.[2]

Historically, a tenant had little protection, if any, from accidentally leasing property that turned out to be uninhabitable. Caveat emptor was the law, and that basically translates to buyers (or renters) beware. Under that maxim, if a consumer leased property without checking it out and later determined that the property was unlivable, the renter would have little legal recourse against the landlord. Eventually, the common law evolved to include an implied warranty of habitability as a measure to protect tenants from unscrupulous landlords.

---

[1] The law often treats business leases differently from residential leases so it is important to note that the lease in this chapter is a residential one. Because it is also a public housing lease, federal laws govern it as well as state and local ones. Another Chapter of this book, Business Acquisitions II, involves a commercial lease.

[2] E.g., Rhode Island requires a landlord to, among other things, (1) Comply with the requirements of applicable building and housing codes affecting health and safety; (2) Make all repairs and do whatever is necessary to put and keep the premises in a fit and habitable condition; (3) Keep all common areas of the premises in a clean and safe condition; (4) Maintain in good and safe working order and condition all electrical, plumbing, sanitary, heating, ventilating, air conditioning, and other facilities and appliances, including elevators, supplied or required to be supplied by him or her. R.I General Laws § 34-18-22 (1987); Delaware law states very specifically what a landlord may and may not do with a tenant's deposit. It allows a landlord to require a deposit but limits the amount to one month's rent, requires that it be placed in an escrow account, and states the purposes of a security deposit to be reimbursement for actual damages beyond normal wear and tear, to repay money owed to the landlord, and to reimburse the landlord for money spent to renovate and re-rent the property caused by a tenant leaving a property before the end of a lease. 25 Del. C. § 7023 (2003). Additionally, twenty-six states have adopted the Uniform Residential Landlord and Tenant Act drafted by the National Conference of Commissioners on Uniform State Laws. The purpose of that act was "to remove the landlord and tenant relationship from the constraints of property law and establish it on the basis of contract with all concomitant rights and remedies." See http://nccusl.org/Update/uniformact_factsheets/uniformacts-fs-urlta.asp

As landlord tenant law developed, so did the form lease. The form lease, like many form contracts, often contains a wide variety of possible clauses for a landlord to pick and choose from. It is not uncommon for a landlord to purchase a form lease from an office supply store or even off of the Internet[3] instead of hiring an attorney to draft a lease for her or his use.

Contract law usually allows parties to shape their own definitions and terms of what their relationship will be with some limitations. Limitations may be found in various federal[4], state, and local, regulations that have evolved to protect tenants from predatory landlords. Additionally, contract law concepts such as unconscionability, misrepresentation, and mistake may be available to police problematic leases.

Recall from your contract studies that when a landlord and tenant sign a lease they are agreeing to a bilateral contract. Each party makes certain promises and a failure to follow through with a promise may result in a breach of the contract/lease, and ultimately may result in the termination of the entire contract. As noted above, in residential leases the local law also may curtail a landlord's ability to simply declare that the lease is at an end and evict the tenant.

SUBSTANTIVE CONTENT:

- Basic Property law concepts

SKILLS AND VALUES UTILIZED:

- Reading and understanding a complex lease.
- Assessing the strengths and weaknesses of a case.
- Writing a complaint for an eviction from a public housing project.

ESTIMATED TIME FOR COMPLETION: Two Hours

LEVEL OF DIFFICULTY (1 to 5):

---

[3] For an example of an internet site that caters to landlords go to: http://www.ezlandlordforms.com. The site claims it is "Trusted by over 40,000 Realtors, Property Managers, Attorneys, and Landlords for all of their professional legal document needs." It has state specific forms for purchase as well as some free forms.

[4] For example the U.S. Department of Housing and Urban Development (HUD) has many rules and regulations that landlords and tenants must follow to be eligible for federal subsidized housing payments.

EXERCISE O:

You work for the local public housing authority in Moped City, (HAMC), and your job requires that you draft legal complaints to evict tenants from their homes. Because the HAMC is a public housing facility that receives federal funds, federal regulations govern its behavior as do state and local rules.

The tenants successfully sued the HAMC a number of years ago for violating their rights on account of substandard housing, routine evictions without good cause, and giving eviction notices with no stated reasons. The publicity over that lawsuit had been the Housing Authority's worst nightmare. The HAMC was raked through the coals for every potential misdeed, real or imagined, that had occurred in the last twenty years.

Since that lawsuit, the HAMC has spent a great deal of time and money to make sure that it provides good and decent living conditions for the tenants. Additionally, it has regulations that require the HAMC to give tenants appropriate notice of problems and evictions. Because one of the findings in the lawsuit against HAMC was that the HAMC routinely evicted tenants without regard for the law or their rights, attorneys for the HAMC drafted a lengthy lease that attempts to articulate with particularity the responsibilities of all of the parties living in or visiting the leased property. Consequently, the HAMC strives to write each eviction notice carefully so it will put the tenant on notice of the objectionable behavior that caused the eviction and each notice now includes the section or sections of the lease that the tenant allegedly violated.

Your supervisor, Susan Longwood, gave you a skimpy file and told you to write an eviction complaint to get Mike Labrador and his family out of their housing unit. She told you that the HAMC had received numerous oral complaints from other tenants about this family over the last year and, although many of them were not documented, the most recent ones are in the file. You asked Susan whether the Labradors had anywhere else to live because you usually tried to refer evicted tenants to a local shelter if they had no other housing. She told you that the local paper reported that Mike's stepfather won a lawsuit against a local department store several months ago for a large amount of damages. As a result, you felt quite certain the Labradors would not be out on the streets if they were evicted. Susan advised you to call the Labrador's home to see if you could get their side of the story. You called several times and left messages but no one returned your calls.

Task One:

Read the complaint from the tenant complaining about the Labrador household, the emergency room report and the other documents that were in the file, reproduced in a folder on the LexisNexis web course. Then read the lease, reproduced below. Begin your work by making a list of the problems the Authority is having with the tenants informed by your brief review of the lease. Be sure to consider the facts in light of the requirements in the lease but focus on the facts that appear to show a breach of the provisions in the lease. For example, if the lease says all lights must be turned off by 9:00 p.m., what do the facts show? Are there complaints that the lights are routinely left on past midnight?

After you have made your list, consult Self-Assessment 1 for Exercise O on the LexisNexis web course.

The Lease between HAMC and the Labradors

PART I   RESIDENTIAL LEASE AGREEMENT: TERMS AND CONDITIONS.[5]

THIS LEASE AGREEMENT (called the lease) is between the Housing Authority of Moped City (herein called HAMC) and Tenants, Mike and Maggie Labrador (herein called Tenant).

I.   Description of the Parties and Premises

   (a)   Premises must be used only as a private residence for Tenant and family members named on Part II of the lease.

   (b)   Any additions to the household members named on the lease, including Live-in Aides and foster children, but excluding natural births, adoptions and court awarded custody, require the advance written approval of HAMC. Such approval will be granted only if the new family members pass HAMC's screening criteria and a unit of the appropriate size is available. Permission to add Live-in Aides and foster children shall not be unreasonably refused.

   (c)   Tenant agrees to wait for HAMC's approval before allowing additional persons to move into the premises. Failure on the part of Tenant to comply with this provision is a serious violation of the material terms of the lease, for which HAMC may terminate the lease in accordance with the regulations stated in this lease.

---

[5]   The two landlord tenant problems are based on a lease between a tenant and a public housing authority. The lease used in the problem is an abbreviated form of the lease actually used by the Housing Authority of Kansas City (HAKC). The rules governing public housing units are somewhat complicated by the fact that it is federal subsidized housing and HUD has the authority to control many of the regulations for the public housing unit. The authors are indebted to Ed Lowndes and Julie Levin for their assistance with this problem. Mr. Lowndes is an attorney and the Executive Director of the Housing Authority of Kansas City and Julie Levin is a Managing Attorney with Legal Aid of Western Missouri. Ms. Levin won the 2009 Kutak-Dodds Prize by the National Legal Aid and Defender Association. The award is given to one attorney every year whose work has promoted the enhancement of human dignity and the quality of life for people who cannot afford legal representation. Ms. Levin won the award due to her commitment to improving public housing in the Kansas City area and her groundbreaking work in public housing issues. She works with the current Executive Director of the HAKC to try to ensure decent public housing for those who cannot afford it in the greater Kansas City area.

II. Rent

    (a) Rent is due and payable in advance on the first day of each month and shall be considered delinquent after the seventh (7th) calendar day of the month. If HAMC makes any changes to the rent, it shall give a minimum of 30 days written notice to Tenant. The notice shall state the new amount, and the date from which the new amount is applicable.

III. Other Charges

    (a) Maintenance costs – The cost for services or repairs due to intentional or negligent damage to the dwelling unit, common area or grounds beyond normal wear and tear, caused by Tenant, household members or by guests.

    (b) When HAMC determines that needed maintenance is not caused by normal wear and tear, Tenant shall be charged for the cost of such service.

    (c) HAMC shall provide written notice of the amount of any charge in addition to Tenant Rent, and when the charge is due. Charges in addition to rent, other than late charges, are due no later than fourteen (14) calendar days after the HAMC gives written notice of the charge.

    (d) Security Deposit

        (a) Tenant Responsibilities: Tenant agrees to pay a security deposit of one month's rent payment not to exceed $ 400.00 except in the case where Tenant is paying a flat rent. In such cases, the flat renter will pay one (1) month rent not to exceed $600.00. The dollar amount of the security deposit is noted on Part II of this Residential Lease. At the option of the HAMC, it may enter into a separate written agreement to gradually accumulate the security deposit. Said agreement must be reasonable based on Tenant's ability to pay. If the Tenant fails to abide by this written agreement the Tenant agrees that it is a serious violation of the lease and termination of tenancy may result.

IV. HAMC's Responsibilities: HAMC will use the Security Deposit at the termination of this Lease:

    (a) To pay the cost of any rent or any other charges owed by Tenant at the termination of this lease.

    (b) To reimburse the cost of repairing any intentional or negligent damages to the dwelling unit caused by Tenant, household members or guests.

    (c) The Security Deposit may not be used to pay rent or other charges while Tenant occupies the dwelling unit. No refund of the Security Deposit will be made until Tenant has vacated, and the HAMC has inspected the dwelling unit.

(d) The return of a security deposit shall occur within thirty (30) days after termination of tenancy. HAMC agrees to return the Security Deposit, if any, to Tenant when he or she vacates, less any deductions for any costs indicated above, and shall mail same to Tenant at the forwarding address, if any, or to the last known address as the case may be. If any deductions are made, HAMC will furnish Tenant, with a written statement of any such costs for damages and/or other charges deducted from the Security Deposit.

V.   Utilities and Appliances

(a) HAMC Paid Utilities: If indicated by an (X) on Part II, HAMC will pay for the indicated utility: electricity, natural gas, heating fuel, water, sewer service, and trash collection. HAMC will not be liable for the failure to supply utility service for any cause whatsoever beyond its control. If indicated by an (X) on the Lease Agreement, HAMC will provide a cooking range and refrigerator. Other major electrical appliances, air conditioners, freezers, extra refrigerators, washers, dryers, etc., may be installed and operated only with the written approval of HAMC.

(b) Tenant-paid Utilities: If Tenant resides in a development where HAMC does not supply electricity, natural gas, heating fuel, water, sewer service, or trash collection, an Allowance for Utilities shall be established, appropriate for the size and type of dwelling unit, for utilities Tenant pays directly to the utility supplier. The total Tenant payment less the Allowance for Utilities equals Tenant rent. If the Allowance for Utilities exceeds the total Tenant payment, HAMC will pay a Utility Reimbursement each month.

(c) HAMC may change the Allowance at any time during the term of the lease, and shall give Tenant sixty (60) days written notice of the revised Allowance along with any resultant changes in Tenant rent or Utility Reimbursement.

(d) If Tenant's actual utility bill exceeds the Allowance for Utilities, Tenant shall be responsible for paying the full actual bill to the supplier. If Tenant's actual utility bill is LESS than the Allowance for Utilities, Tenant shall receive the benefit of such saving.

VI. Tenant Responsibilities

(a) Tenant Responsibilities: Tenant agrees not to waste the utilities provided by HAMC and to comply with any applicable law, regulation, or guideline of any governmental entity regulating utilities or fuels.

(b) Tenant also agrees to abide by any local ordinance or House Rules restricting or prohibiting the use of space heaters in multi-dwelling units.

VII. Terms and Conditions:

The following terms and conditions of occupancy are made a part of the Lease:

(a) Use and Occupancy of Dwelling: Tenant shall have the right to exclusive use and occupancy of the dwelling unit for Tenant and other household members listed on the lease. With the prior written consent of HAMC, a member of the household may engage in legal profit-making activities in the dwelling unit.

This provision permits reasonable accommodation of Tenant's guests or visitors for a period not exceeding fourteen (14) days each year. Permission may be granted, upon written request to the Manager, for an extension of this provision.

(b) Ability to comply with Lease terms: If, during the term of this Lease, Tenant, by reason of physical or mental impairment is no longer able to comply with the material provisions of this lease, and cannot make arrangements for someone to aid him/her in complying with the lease, and HAMC cannot make any reasonable accommodation that would enable Tenant to comply with the lease; HAMC will assist Tenant, or designated Member(s) of Tenant's family, to find more suitable housing and move Tenant from the dwelling unit at Tenant's expense. If there are no family members who can or will take responsibility for moving Tenant, HAMC will work with appropriate agencies to secure suitable housing and will terminate the Lease.

At the time of admission, all Tenants must identify the family member(s) to be contacted if they become unable to comply with lease terms.

(c) Rent Adjustments: Tenant will be notified in writing of any rent adjustment due to the conditions described above; all notices will state the effective date of the rent adjustment.

(1) In the event of a rent decrease, the adjustment will become effective on the first day of the month following the reported change in circumstances, provided Tenant reported the change in a timely manner, as specified above.

(2) In the case of a rent increase, when an increase in income occurs after a prior rent reduction and is

reported within 10 calendar days of the occurrence, the increase will become effective the first day of the 2nd month following the month in which the change was reported.

(3) In the case of a rent increase due to misrepresentation, failure to report a change in family composition, or failure to report an increase in income (after a reduction in rent per the fixed rent policy), HAMC shall apply the increase in rent retroactive to the first of the month following the month in which the misrepresentation occurred.

VIII. Other Responsibilities

HAMC shall be obligated:

(a) To maintain the dwelling unit and the development in decent, safe and sanitary condition;

(b) To comply with the requirements of applicable building codes, housing codes, and HUD regulations materially affecting health and safety;

(c) To make necessary repairs to the dwelling unit;

(d) To keep the building, facilities, and common areas, not otherwise accessed by Tenant for maintenance and upkeep, in a clean and safe condition;

(e) To maintain in good and safe working order and condition electrical, plumbing, sanitary, heating, ventilating, and other facilities and appliances; including elevators supplied or required to be supplied with HAMC;

(f) Where applicable, to provide and maintain appropriate receptacles and facilities (except containers for the exclusive use of an individual tenant family) for the deposit of garbage, rubbish, and other waste removed from the premise by Tenant as required by this Lease;

(g) To supply running water and reasonable amounts of hot water and reasonable amount of heat at appropriate times of the year according to local custom and usage; EXCEPT where the building that includes the dwelling unit is not required to be equipped for that purpose, or where heat or hot water is generated by an installation within the exclusive control of Tenant and supplied by a direct utility connection;

(h) To notify Tenant of the specific grounds for any proposed adverse action by HAMC. (Such adverse action includes, but is not limited to: a proposed lease termination, transfer of Tenant to another unit, change in amount of rent, or imposition of charges for maintenance and repair, or for excess use of utilities.) When HAMC is required to afford Tenant the opportunity for a hearing under the HAMC grievance procedure for a grievance concerning a proposed adverse action it will so advise the Tenant.

Tenant shall be obligated:

(i) To act in a cooperative manner with neighbors and HAMC Staff. To refrain from and cause members of Tenant's household or guests to refrain from acting or speaking in an abusive or threatening manner toward neighbors and HAMC staff.

(j) Not to illegally display, use, or possess or allow members of Tenant's household or guests to illegally display, use, or possess any firearms or other illegal weapons as defined by the laws and courts of Dakota anywhere on the property of HAMC.

(k) To take reasonable precautions to prevent fires and to refrain from storing or keeping highly volatile or flammable materials upon the premises. Tenant shall not use a grill within fifteen (15) feet of the residence.

(l) To avoid obstructing sidewalks, areaways, galleries, passages, elevators, or stairs and to avoid using these for purposes other than going in and out of the dwelling unit.

(m) To refrain from erecting or hanging radio, or television antennas, or satellite dishes on or from any part of the dwelling unit or building without prior written approval of the property manager.

(n) To refrain from placing signs of any type on or about the dwelling unit without prior written approval of the property manager.

(o) To refrain from, and cause members of Tenant's household to refrain from keeping, maintaining, harboring, or boarding any animal of any nature in the dwelling unit except in accordance with HAMC's pet policy.

(p) To assure that Tenant, any member of the household, a guest, or another person under Tenant's control, shall not engage in:

(1) Any criminal activity that threatens the safety, or right to peaceful enjoyment of HAMC's public housing premises by other residents or employees of HAMC or;

(2) Any drug-related criminal activity. Any criminal activity in violation of the preceding sentence shall be cause for termination of tenancy, and for eviction from the unit for the purposes of this lease, the term drug-related criminal activity means the illegal possession,

manufacture, sale, distribution, use or possession with intent to manufacture, sell, distribute, or use, any controlled substance as defined in Section 102 of the Controlled Substances Act.

(q) It shall be presumed that any individual who is listed on this lease as a member of the Tenant's household, and who engages in criminal activity, resides with the Resident unless, before the date of any incident giving rise to criminal activity, Tenant shall specifically inform the property management in writing that said individual is no longer a member of his/her household, no longer resides upon the leased premises, and requests removal of that individual from the lease.

(r) It shall be presumed that any individual who engages in criminal activity is a guest, visitor, or person under the Tenant's control if the Tenant knew or should have known of the criminal activity. The Tenant shall immediately report any person residing in the unit, as well as any guest, visitor or person under the Tenant's control engaging in criminal activity and/or that the Tenant cannot supervise and control. Reporting activity and following through with documentation of the event shall constitute a defense for the Tenant. Failure to report the activity constitutes a waiver by the Tenant of lack of control as a defense to any action taken by HAMC under this section, unless the Tenant had no prior knowledge of the criminal activity.

IX. Termination of the Lease and Notice

In terminating the Lease, the following procedures shall be followed by HAMC and Tenant:

(a) This Lease may be terminated for serious or repeated violations of material terms of the Lease including, but not limited to, failure to make payments due under the lease or to fulfill Tenant obligations set forth in Section VII above, or for other good cause. If the Tenant fails to vacate the premises after termination of the lease and, if applicable, after unsuccessfully appealing the matter through the grievance hearing process, the HAMC may file an appropriate court action against the Tenant and, if the Tenant loses said lawsuit, then Tenant shall be required to pay HAMC's costs such as court costs and a reasonable attorney's fee to HAMC.

(b) Such serious or repeated violation of terms shall include but not be limited to:

1. The failure to pay rent or other payments when due;

2. The failure to pay delinquent rent as discussed above by the last day of the month in which the rent is delinquent;

X. Grievance Procedure - In accordance with the applicable Federal regulations, HAMC's Grievance Procedure shall be applicable to all individual grievances (as defined in the Grievance Procedure) between Tenant and the HAMC with the following exception:

> HUD has issued a due process determination that the law of the State of Dakota requires that a Tenant be given the opportunity for a hearing in court, which provides the basic elements of due process before eviction from the dwelling unit. Thus, when approved or authorized by senior management personnel, the grievance procedure shall not be required of any termination of tenancy or eviction that involves:

(a) (1) Any criminal activity that is an imminent threat to the health or safety of residents or employees of the HAMC, or

(2) Any violent or serious drug-related criminal activity on or off HAMC's premises.

(b) There will, however, be a presumption that all tenants are entitled to a grievance hearing unless there is clear evidence that the eviction involves activity stated in (1) or (2) above and senior management personnel has approved the exclusion of a grievance hearing.

(c) HAMC shall give prior written notice of the proposed lease termination date as set forth below. The time frames listed below will begin on the earliest of either: the date that the notice is delivered to the tenant OR the date that the notice is placed in the United States mail, first class, postage prepaid, to wit:

(i) Fourteen (14) days in the case of failure to pay rent;

(ii) A reasonable time, considering the seriousness of the situation (but not to exceed 30 days) when the health or safety of other tenants or HAMC staff is threatened; if any member of the household has engaged in any drug-related or violent criminal activity; or if any member of the household has been convicted of a felony; or

(iii) One full calendar month in any other case unless Dakota law allows for a shorter time period.

(d) The notice of termination:

(1) The notice of termination to Tenant shall state specific reasons for the termination, shall inform Tenant of his/her right to make such reply as he/she may wish, and Tenant's right to examine HAMC documents directly relevant to the termination or eviction.

(2) When HAMC is required to offer Tenant the opportunity for a hearing, the notice shall also inform Tenant of the right to request such a hearing in accordance with the HAMC's grievance procedures.

(3) Any notice to vacate (or to quit) that is required by State or local law may be combined with, or run concurrently with the notice of lease termination under this section. The Notice to Vacate must be in writing, and specify that if Tenant fails to vacate (or to quit) the premises within the statutory period then an appropriate court action will be brought against the Tenant and if the Tenant loses said lawsuit then Tenant shall be required to pay court costs and a reasonable attorney's fee.

(4) When HAMC is required to offer Tenant the opportunity for a grievance hearing concerning the lease termination under HAMC's grievance procedure, the tenancy shall not terminate (even if any Notice to Vacate under State or local law has expired) until the period to request a hearing has expired, or (if a hearing is requested) the grievance process has been completed.

(5) When HAMC is not required to offer Tenant the opportunity for a hearing under the grievance procedure and HAMC has decided to exclude such grievance from HAMC grievance procedure, the notice of lease termination shall (a) state that Tenant is not entitled to a grievance hearing on the termination; (b) specify the judicial eviction procedure to be used by HAMC for eviction and state that HAMC has determined that this eviction procedure provides the opportunity for a hearing in a court that contains the basic elements of due process, and (c) state whether the eviction is for a criminal activity that is an imminent threat to the health or safety of residents or employees of the HAMC or any violent or serious drug-related criminal activity on or off HAMC's premises.

(6) HAMC may evict Tenant from the unit only by bringing a court action.

(e) Tenant may terminate this Lease at any time by giving at least one full calendar month advance written notice to HAMC prior to the actual date that Tenant intends to vacate, consistent with the procedure as described in this lease.

(f) In deciding to evict for criminal activity, HAMC shall have discretion to consider all of the circumstances of the case, including the seriousness of the offense, the extent of participation by or awareness of family members, and the effects that the eviction would have both on family members not involved in the proscribed activity and on the family's neighbors. In appropriate cases, HAMC may permit continued occupancy by remaining family members and may impose a condition that family members who engaged in the proscribed activity will neither reside in nor visit the unit. HAMC may require a family member who has engaged in the illegal use of drugs to present credible evidence of successful completion of a treatment program, as a condition to being allowed to reside in the unit.

XI. Waiver

No delay or failure by HAMC in exercising any right under this lease agreement, and no partial or single exercise of any such right shall constitute a waiver of that or any other right, unless otherwise expressly provided herein.

PART II: RESIDENTIAL LEASE AGREEMENT

THIS AGREEMENT is executed between the Housing Authority of Moped City, Dakota (herein called "HAMC") and Mike and Maggie Labrador (herein called the "Tenant"). It becomes effective as of this date Sept. 1, 0000.

(1) Unit: The HAMC, relying upon the representations of Tenant as to Tenant's income, household composition and housing need, leases to Tenant, (upon Terms and Conditions set forth in this Lease agreement) the dwelling unit LOCATED at (and hereinafter called the "premises") to be occupied exclusively as a private residence by Tenant and household. The Tenant unit number/address is:

368 Athena Drive, Riverdale Unit 608

(2) Household Composition: The Tenant's household is composed of the individuals listed below. (Other than the Head or Spouse, each household member should be listed by age, oldest to youngest. All members of the household over age 18 shall execute the lease.)

Name	Age
Mike Labrador	26
Maggie Labrador	25
Stella Labrador	8
Joe Labrador	6

(3) Term: The term of this lease shall be one calendar year, renewed as stipulated in Part 1 of the Lease for the period beginning and ending at midnight on August, 31, 0000.

(4) Rent: Initial rent (prorated for partial month if necessary) shall be $ 600.

(5) Thereafter, rent in the amount of $ 600 per month shall be payable in advance on the first day of each month, and shall be delinquent after the seventh (7th) calendar day of said month.

This is the flat rent for the unit based upon the income and other information provided by the Tenant.

(6) Utilities and Appliances: HAMC-Supplied Utilities If indicated by an (X) below. HAMC provides the indicated utility as part of the rent for the premises:
(X) Electricity ( ) Natural Gas ( ) Heating Fuel (X) Water (X) Sewerage ( ) Other

If indicated by an (X) below, HAMC shall provide the following appliances for the premises:

Cooking Range   (X)

Refrigerator   (X)

Dishwasher   ( )

(7) Utility Allowances: Tenant-Paid Utilities If indicated by an (X) below, HAKC shall provide Tenant with a Utility Allowance in the monthly amount totaling $N/A for the following utilities paid directly by the Tenant to the Utility supplier.
( ) Electricity ( ) Gas ( ), Heat ( ) Water ( ) Sewerage ( ) Trash removal ( ) Tenant's cooking range ( ) Tenant-supplied refrigerator

(8) Charges for Excess Appliances are not applicable to tenants who pay utilities directly to utility Supplier. Charges for excess appliances are due for the following:

(i) Air Conditioners: An additional charge of $ 50 per month will be payable for each air conditioner on the premises for each month of occupancy.

(ii) Other Appliances: If checked below, an additional charge of $15 per month for each month of occupancy for each excess appliance on the premises.

( ) Freezer, type

( ) Extra Refrigerator

( ) Second color TV

( ) Second Stereo

( ) Automatic washer

( ) Electric space heater

( ) Other: If other, state the name of the appliance.

(9) Security Deposit: Tenant agrees to pay the sum of $600 as a security deposit and by signing below the HAMC and Tenant agree that said sum has been paid to the HAMC.

/s/ *Mike and Maggie Labrador*

Task Two:

Now, examine the lease in more detail against the list of problems. Which parts of the lease are relevant to your job of drafting the eviction complaint? Make a list of the paragraphs and, if they are relevant, indicate the relevance. This requires you to match facts that are relevant to specific terms in the lease and then use your judgment as to whether the lease was breached. Then consult Self-Assessment 2 for Exercise O on the LexisNexis web course.

Task Three:

Equipped with your analysis of the problems and the lease provisions that are relevant to your drafting task, please draft an eviction complaint that will comply with the Authority's obligations under the lease. The complaint and allegations should track the violations of the lease. For now, do not consider other laws that might complicate the eviction proceeding. Consult Self-Assessment 3 for Exercise O on the LexisNexis web course.

Chapter 16

READING A LEASE CONTRACT AND DRAFTING AN ARBITRATION MEMORANDUM

PREVIEW

In this Chapter you will review a file that contains a lease contract, a complaint from a tenant who was seriously injured by one of your clients, an emergency room report, and file notes concerning complaints from other tenants. You also will have facts from your client, which, as you can imagine, tell a different story. The landlord, a public housing authority, has issued your client an eviction notice and your client desires to remain in their home. The housing authority has established a pre-litigation method to resolve conflicts, when possible, using a non-binding arbitration proceeding. Generally, if tenants are successful at the arbitration level, the housing authority will not attempt further eviction proceedings. You will need to write an arbitration memorandum, which is a persuasive statement of facts on behalf of your client, to submit to the arbitrator.[1]

SKILLS AND VALUES UTILIZED:

- Reading and interpreting a lease contract.
- Assessing the strengths and weaknesses of a case.
- Writing a memorandum of facts from opposing sides.

---

[1] **Sidebar on Contractual Arbitration.** As you may know, contracting parties can agree to submit either a pending or later dispute to an arbitrator for resolution. There is much debate about "pre-dispute arbitration" agreements when the so-called "agreement" is embedded in small print that a customer receives from a vendor with the monthly bill (called "bill stuffers" by critics). But if the arbitration agreement is sound, most courts will require the parties to resolve their dispute the way the contract requires. In many cases, the arbitration provision will specify an arbitration services vendor and may either specify or incorporate rules to govern the proceedings.

Most contractual arbitration is "binding" meaning that the results are, for all intents and purposes, final. A federal statute, the Federal Arbitration Act (9 U.S.C. § 1 *et seq.*) requires courts to enforce contractual arbitration provisions as vigorously as other contract provisions and severely limits rights to proceed in court following an arbitration award. Arbitration that is, by agreement, "non-binding" escapes these restrictions. As its name suggests, the parties are *not* bound by the arbitrator's decision because they did not agree to be bound by it. In that respect, non-binding arbitration is essentially advisory in nature, giving the parties a chance to see what a neutral party thinks of their case but not binding them to that decision. One suspects that, in many cases, this advances the odds that the parties will settle their case voluntarily. Mediation is another dispute resolution process that is non-binding but in mediation, the mediator acts as a facilitator for the parties' negotiation and does not issue a decision as an arbitrator would in non-binding arbitration.

ESTIMATED TIME FOR COMPLETION: Two Hours

LEVEL OF DIFFICULTY (1 to 5):

INTRODUCTION TO EXERCISE P:

This is a continuation of the problem from Chapter 15, **Drafting a Public Housing Eviction Complaint Based on Breach of a Lease**, involving the Labrador family, though you can do this exercise without doing the other. The Labradors have lived in public housing for several years. The housing is owned and managed by the Housing Authority of Moped City (HAMC). Although tenants had successfully sued HAMC in the past over the housing and HAMC's procedures, it has always strived to provide decent affordable housing for low-income families.

In Exercise O, the Labradors started having troubles with their neighbors about six months ago. Maggie Labrador (the wife) has some mental health issues. As her mental health deteriorated, Maggie became involved in numerous arguments with her neighbors and those arguments escalated on two occasions into physical confrontations with her neighbors. The culmination of these problems occurred when Maggie argued with a neighbor, Marla Johnson, and that argument ended when Maggie stabbed Marla with a knife. The injury was serious enough that Marla was taken to the Emergency Room where the doctors had to use 23 stitches to close the wound. After that incident, Marla Johnson wrote a lengthy complaint against the Labrador family that ultimately led to the HAMC deciding to evict the Labradors from their public housing apartment. Mike, the husband, says they will be homeless if they are evicted from their home.

EXERCISE P:

Once again, the pro bono coordinator in your firm, Pete Shepherd, has asked you for assistance with a case he recently received from the local Volunteer Attorney Program (VAP). Pete always pre-screens the cases that come in through the VAP program and he tries to select attorneys who have an interest in the problem area presented by the client. Because Pete knew that you had significant issues with a landlord while you were in law school (which is something you have been quite vocal about), he asked you to take the case and you agreed to do so.

Pete told you that the client, Mike Labrador, is married and has two children. His wife has had serious mental health problems and consequently has been in and out of mental health institutions during the last year. Mike has been working two jobs to try to make ends meet and living in public housing. He is a dishwasher at a local restaurant and he obtains temporary work whenever possible. Because of this, he has never missed his rent or been late with a payment.

According to Pete, Mike and his family have had several problems with his neighbors in the past and Mike has had what he describes as a couple of "run-ins" with the management of his public housing unit. He recently received an eviction notice from the public housing unit where he lives with his family. Pete told you that Mike cannot afford other kinds of housing and, if he is evicted from his apartment, he fears the family will become homeless. He said that a short time ago there was an article in the newspaper about Gerald Jordan, Mike's stepfather, reporting that Mr. Jordan had received a large money judgment in a lawsuit against a local department store. Mike's mother recently divorced his stepfather and Gerald and Mike have not been on speaking terms for several years, so Pete feels quite certain that the newly-wealthy stepfather will not come to Mike's rescue.

After getting all this from Pete, you interviewed Mike and discovered a little more information. Mike told you that when he first moved into public housing, his wife and two children were living with him. According to Mike, his wife Maggie has had serious mental health problems in the last two years and that has caused difficulties in the housing complex. She used to yell at him, the children, and the neighbors and make a lot of noise late at night. Neighbors were constantly complaining and Mike said that it caused a great deal of friction between his family and other tenants in the building. He did say, however, that Marla Johnson their neighbor across the hall has caused more problems than they have. Mike told you that Marla knew Maggie had mental health problems; yet, Marla constantly harassed her and tried to pick fights. He stated that it was almost always Marla, not Maggie, who started the fights. Additionally, Mike told you that the "stabbing incident" began when Marla first threw a can of beans at Maggie while Maggie was holding a knife she was using to prepare dinner and that the stabbing was an accident.

One year ago, Maggie's brother, Joseph moved into the same public housing complex where the Labradors live. According to Mike, Joseph is the "craziest person he has ever met who is not in an institution." Unfortunately, Maggie and Joseph do not get along. They fought every time they saw each other. The arguments were so volatile that the neighbors filed a number of complaints against both families. Joseph vandalized several apartments, including the Labrador's, by writing profanity on the doors and breaking into the apartment when no one was home. Mike said that Marla's home was vandalized that way and she always blamed it on Maggie, even though Maggie was not involved. Eventually, Joseph was evicted from the housing complex for his responsibility in vandalizing apartments. Around this time, Maggie was institutionalized.

According to Mike, his neighbors blame him for many of the problems caused by his wife and her brother because they thought he should have referred his wife to social services sooner, so she could have gotten the help she needed. What the neighbors do not know is that Mike had referred Maggie to social services previously on numerous occasions and he had even signed the papers to have her involuntarily committed twice. That caused a complete breakdown in his family and Mike told you that his wife and her family never forgave him for signing the papers to have Maggie involuntarily committed. His wife and her family have always believed that the family should have worked all this out on their own. The neighbors also thought he should have done something to stop his brother in law from vandalizing apartments and causing other problems in the building but Mike said that was ridiculous since he had absolutely no control over Joseph.

Mike told you that, of course, nothing is as easy as it seems and he had to take his children's lives into account. According to Mike, Maggie's entire family has serious mental health issues ranging from schizophrenia to bipolar disorder to severe depression. He told you that he loves his wife and he had hoped that she could get help on an out-patient basis but she often would not follow through with taking her medicine. He said that, although he now realizes it was an unrealistic goal to believe that Maggie could be treated as an out-patient, this belief is the basis for much of the acrimony between him, his neighbors, and the housing authority.

After a month of being institutionalized, Maggie was released to a half way house about ½ mile from the housing complex where Mike lives with his two children. Several weeks ago, Maggie stopped by the house to visit with her family. Mike reported that the visit went well, the children were thrilled to see their mother, and she returned to the half way home the same day. Although there were no incidents during that visit, Mike heard that a neighbor had filed a complaint against the Labradors saying they had a violent family member living in the house and that was against HAMC rules. He thinks it is his neighbor across the hall who, according to Mike, simply does not like Maggie.

Last week, Maggie stopped by the house again to see Mike and the children. She stayed overnight because there was bad weather and he could tell that the children were very happy to see their mother again and did not want her to leave. The next morning, a Saturday, Mike went to work and left Maggie at home with the children. Several hours later a neighbor across the hall, Brian Jones, stopped by the apartment. Unfortunately, that visit turned into an altercation and, according to Maggie and both of her children, it was Brian who caused the problems. He accused Maggie of having written derogatory sayings on his apartment door. Maggie responded by throwing a book at him. The police were called and both Maggie and Brian were taken to the police station to "cool off," although neither of them was charged. Maggie subsequently refused to return to the halfway house and moved back home.

Two days later, Maggie was at home and was having a hard time controlling the children. Mike says that he honestly does not know what happened but the situation rapidly deteriorated. Although he does not know why his neighbor Marla Johnson came to the apartment that day, he knows that "there is no love lost" between Marla and Maggie. According to Maggie, Marla started to yell at her and tell her she had no business being in the housing complex because she was cruel to her children and a nut. According to Mike, Marla was so confrontational that she yelled at Maggie for several minutes and threw a can of beans at her. That totally sent Maggie off of the deep end. Unfortunately, that deep end involved a large butcher knife.

The next week Mike received a notice from the manager stating that he had 30 days to vacate his apartment. Mike told you that he couldn't lose his apartment because he, Maggie, and their two children have nowhere else to live. He said Maggie had moved back home with the approval of her doctors, started taking her medication regularly, and was being careful to avoid the neighbors and not get into any arguments.

The grievance procedure that the parties agreed to through the lease contract has a special process that allows both sides to submit a statement to an arbitrator for a proposed settlement of the dispute. The arbitrator is randomly drawn from a list of people who have been approved by the housing authority and the tenant's association. Although the arbitrator's decision is not binding on either the HAMC or the tenant, the HMAC usually abides by the ruling. You know if you can win at the non-binding arbitration level that there is a 90% chance the HAMC will allow your client to continue living in the public housing unit.

Task One:

Assume that the notice of appeal from the eviction has been filed. After you filed the appeal, you were provided with the HAMC's file on the Labrador family. This included the lease, the complaint, and the notations in the file relating to communications between the HAMC and the Labradors. The eviction notice is reprinted in the next paragraph and the lease is reprinted in Chapter 15. You need to review these documents[2] and the rules governing the arbitration that are located at the end of this task.

Your job is to write a memorandum of facts for the Labradors — no longer than 2 pages — that succinctly states why the Labrador family should not be removed from their apartment by the public housing

---

[2] The rest of these documents are in the HAMC v. Labrador Folder on the LexisNexis web course.

authority. Remember that your goal is to get the HAMC to allow Mike and his family to remain in their home and your best chance of doing that is by winning the non-binding arbitration. Thus, you will need to write a persuasive memorandum supported by the facts and the law.

EVICTION NOTICE

To: Mike and Maggie Labrador
Re: Eviction from 368 Athena Drive, Riverdale Unit 608
Date: 00/00/0000

Dear Mr. And Mrs. Labrador this letter is your notice to quit and vacate the property rented to you located at 368 Athena Drive, Riverdale Unit 608. The HAMC has notified you on a number of occasions of objectionable behavior by members of your family that has caused problems in the Riverdale Housing Unit. Specifically, you have been notified personally of complaints from your neighbors, constant arguing with your neighbors, and being so loud that you bother your neighbors. The culmination of these arguments resulted in two serious incidents: first, Maggie Labrador assaulted Brian Jones by throwing a book at him and second, she violently assaulted Marla Johnson by stabbing her with a knife. This last incident was so severe that it resulted in Marla having to be taken to the emergency room where she needed 23 stitches to close the wound in her arm.

You have violated Section VIII of your lease by refusing to cooperate with your neighbors, being belligerent to your neighbors, and committing violent criminal acts against your neighbors. The HAMC has warned you repeatedly; yet you have not fixed these problems. Instead, they have escalated. Furthermore, you failed to report any of this criminal activity to the HAMC's main office as required by Section VIII of your lease. Therefore, you have 30 days to vacate your apartment. You have a right to respond to this notice but that response must be delivered to our office within 30 days.

You also have the right to appeal this eviction by using the grievance process established in your lease if you believe these charges are not valid and you have a defense to them. A request for a grievance hearing may delay your departure from the housing unit. If, however, the HAMC has to start an eviction proceeding against you in a court of law you ultimately may be required to pay attorneys fees in the event that you lose the case.

Because there have been some allegations about the mental health of your wife, the HAMC will try to work with you to find alternate housing if you desire. Please let us know if you want assistance in relocating.

A request for a grievance hearing must be made within 14 days.

/S/ Dudley Doolittle

RULES GOVERNING ARBITRATION MEMORANDUM

(1) Within one week, after filing an appeal from an eviction notice, each party may submit an arbitration memorandum.

(2) The arbitration memorandum is a statement of facts from your client's perspective. It should be no longer than two (2) pages. It should summarize the nature of the matter and the tenant's (or HAMC's) position on the major factual issues affecting the eviction. This memorandum should reference any relevant sections of the lease.

(3) The Arbitration Memorandum is solely for use in the arbitration process and shall not be filed in a court of law.

After completing your memorandum of facts, consult Self-Assessment 1 for Exercise P on the LexisNexis web course.

Task Two:

Now imagine that you are the attorney for the HAMC and the Executive Director, Joe Tyler, has directed you to remove the Labradors from public housing. He fears repercussions from other tenants as well as the media, if the Labradors are permitted to continue living in their apartment. Joe told you that he has received a message from an attorney named Steve Rudd who claims to represent Marla Johnson. Mr. Rudd threatened to sue HAMC for his client's injuries if the Labradors stay in the apartment building.

Write a memorandum for the HAMC — no longer than 2 pages — that succinctly states why Mike and his family should be removed from the public housing. You should follow the rules governing the Arbitration Memorandum that are printed in Task One.

After you have written your answer, consult Self-Assessment 2 for Exercise P on the LexisNexis web course.